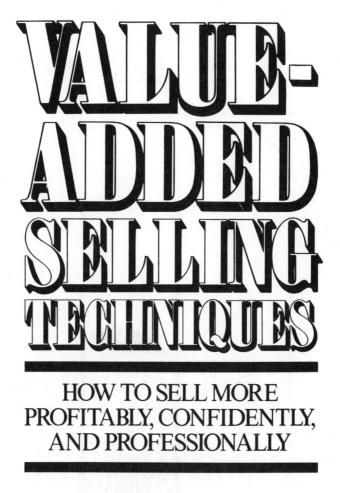

VALUE-ADDED SELLING TECHNIQUES

HOW TO SELL MORE PROFITABLY, CONFIDENTLY, AND PROFESSIONALLY

TOM REILLY

CONGDON & WEED, INC.
Chicago

Library of Congress Cataloging-in-Publication Data

Reilly, Thomas P.
     Value-added selling techniques : how to sell more profitably,
confidently, and professionally / Tom Reilly.
          p.   cm.
     ISBN 0-86553-205-2
     1. Selling.   I. Title.
HF5438.25.R45   1989
658.8′5—dc19   89-30188
                                                                           CIP

Published by Congdon & Weed, Inc.
A subsidiary of Contemporary Books, Inc.
Two Prudential Plaza, Chicago, Illinois 60601-6790
Manufactured in the United States of America
International Standard Book Number: 0-86553-205-2
                                        0-8092-0505-2z
                                        Contemporary Books, Inc.
99 00 01 02 03 BH 18 17 16 15 14 13 12

Contents

To my parents, John and Mossie Reilly, whose love ignited my self-confidence and strengthened my vision to see beyond human limitations

Introduction

Congratulations! I'll bet you don't know you enjoy the distinction of belonging to an elite group of super-achievers. You are doing something at this moment that fewer than 10 percent of your peers will do this year—reading a book on sales. In my seminars, I ask for a show of hands from those people who remember the last sales book they read. Fewer than 10 percent—actually, closer to 5 percent—raise their hands. I'm convinced that it's the unique combination of your initiative and their inertia that will create the success you desire.

In writing this book, I made some assumptions about your selling needs. For example, I assumed:

- You're in a price-sensitive market. Price may not be the only variable, but it is a significant buying criterion for your customers.
- You're frustrated, perplexed, haunted, and taunted by these five words: "Your price is too high!"
- "I want to get two more competitive bids!" chafes you.

1

- You are dismayed at "Our budget is committed for the rest of the year!"
- You have more competition than you want.
- Your profit margins erode with each competitive thrust.
- You're caught in a dilemma. Your boss wants you to increase sales, and the buyer wants you to decrease prices.

Let's take this a step further. I've assumed these are your objectives in purchasing this book:

- You want to gain a substantial competitive edge over any and all of your competitors.
- You want some practical ideas on what to do when the buyer resists your price offer.
- You want to learn the fine art of getting your buyer to think in terms of value rather than price.
- Mostly, you want some practical ideas on how to sell products or services for more profit.

If you answered "Yes" to any of the above, this book is for you. If you answered "Yes" to several of the above statements, this is a tailor-made success manual for you!

We share a common goal. My goal is to teach you how to become more creative, tenacious, and persuasive. When that happens, you'll be selling more profitably because you'll be embracing a value-oriented sales philosophy which serves as the foundation for this book.

Value-oriented selling is a philosophy which acknowledges that two sets of needs exist in any sale. Your buyer has a need to solve a problem, and you have a need to sell a product for a profit. It's a mutual profit objective. The buyer doesn't want to be gouged, and you want to turn a fair gain. In a value-oriented sales environment, both of you achieve your goals. Your desire to sell profitably isn't dwarfed by your concern for the buyer's needs. If you are concerned for both sets of needs, you embrace a value-oriented sales philosophy. The value-oriented salesperson constantly looks for ways to enhance his product, service, or company for his buyer while preserving the integrity of his margins. To achieve this, he uses value-added selling techniques. We begin with a simple philosophy and then develop skills that are consistent with this philosophy. That's what this book is all about.

Prepare yourself for an educational journey unlike anything you've experienced in the past. You'll marvel at the many wonders along the way—marvels like the magic of the value-added sales call (planning, implementation, and follow-up), the secrets for avoiding price objections, the master rebuttal techniques to neutralize price resistance, the powerful negotiating concepts for salespeople, the logic of when/how to raise prices, and the discovery of how to "hug your customer."

When you embrace this value-oriented philosophy and use these value-added selling techniques, you make a strong commitment. You're making a commitment to your company by leveraging your sales time well. You're pursuing your duty to sell more profitably. You're making a commitment to your buyer to find the best way to solve his problem. Beyond that, you're making a commitment to actively seek ways to increase the value of your offering to him. You're also making a commitment to yourself. You're committing to a standard of excellence that accepts nothing less than the best you can give—a commitment to realizing the performance potential that lies within you. Value-oriented selling is the philosophy, and *Value-Adding Selling Techniques* is the method. Good luck with your commitment and your journey.

1
Value-Added Selling

Value is in the eye of the beholder. It's a perception driven by needs, wants, and desires. What's valuable for you is not necessarily valuable for me. In sales, value is simply the way in which the buyer's needs interface with your product. If your product and services have much in common with the buyer's needs and situational variables, it's a good value for the buyer.

Mark Twain said, "It's the differences of opinion that give us a horse race!" I think he had buying and selling in mind when he coined this expression. A college student operating on a limited budget finds greater value in a discount, no-frills airfare with a box lunch than a business executive who flies a hundred thousand miles each year. Value is determined by the buyer's unique set of factors. Some he is aware of—others he is not.

We could debate all day in esoteric terms the value of something. We could discuss intrinsic and extrinsic value. We could even rely on philosophical commentaries by sixteenth century economists. In sales, the impact your product has on the buyer's needs determines its value. The greater the buyer's awareness of these needs, the greater the potential value of your product. If the buyer perceives a need only for a good price, it's incumbent upon you to raise his awareness that other needs exist and then create buyer desire to satisfy these needs. Value means a great many things to a buyer rather than just a good price. It means dollars saved in the long run, increased revenues, convenience, safety, better delivery, among other things. Raise his awareness that value encompasses all of this and more. Awaken his interest through probing for needs and satisfying those needs with benefits. Explain how your company delivers this value.

Selling profitably is a major goal of all companies. Even nonprofit organizations must earn profit to break even. Selling profitably requires that you fully understand value-added selling and the impact cutting your price has on your company. In this chapter we'll explore these issues and then examine some interesting facts about price.

WHY DON'T SALESPEOPLE SELL MORE?

If the value-added selling philosophy makes sense, why don't more salespeople do it? This is an especially relevant question. Based on my experiences and what I hear in seminars, there are several reasons for this.

First, the salesperson may feel guilty selling at a higher price. This occurs because the salesperson feels uneasy charging more for a product when he knows there's flexibility built into the pricing structure. He finds himself fretting over "gouging" one of his existing customers. He may even start worrying, "Gee, what happens if they find out I could have discounted but didn't?" or "What if my customer discovers that he could have gotten a better price from another vendor or that another customer paid less for the same item?" If the salesperson is a price shopper in his own buying habits, he'll feel guilty charging the customer more than the maximum discount.

Second, the salesperson may not understand the value

that his company delivers, misunderstand the true value of his product, or fail to grasp the concept of value-added selling. If the salesperson doesn't understand it, he's unlikely to sell it. A lack of skills may also inhibit a salesperson's emphasizing value-added selling. Perhaps no one has ever taught him how to sell the concept. Plain and simple— he just doesn't know how.

Third, if a salesperson is too hungry for business, he may cut the price because he doesn't want to lose the order. It's too risky, in his opinion, to sell at a higher price. His thought is, "Why run the risk of losing the business over a matter of additional profit? We're still doing OK on this order!" He may feel that "10 percent of something is better than 20 percent of nothing." That might be true depending on the situation. Discounting must be strategic—not accidental!

Fourth, a salesperson may not sell value because it requires a lot of effort. It's much easier to fit the order-taker mode than the order-maker mode. It's the path of least resistance. Do what's easy and simple. This is reactive selling versus proactive selling. It's a "get the business and run"–type philosophy: "We'll make it up on the next one!"

Finally, the customer may do a better job of selling the salesperson than the salesperson does of selling the customer. The customer persuades the salesperson that the only way they will be able to do business is at the lower price. It's a take-it-or-leave-it situation.

Selling value is a process. It's not a one-time event with the customer. It's a way of life, a mindset for salespeople. Most have discovered it's a profitable and successful lifestyle. It's a way to enrich your sales career while providing maximum return to the customer.

THE VALUE-ADDED SALES APPROACH

Historically, "value-added" is a concept in which one company purchases the raw materials and does something to these materials that adds value to the buyer. This could be a manufacturer of commodity products or a distributor of highly differentiated products, or anything in between. "Value-added" refers to how the manufacturer or distributor changes, enhances, or improves the basic product to increase its value to the buyer.

Value-added selling is built around a value-oriented philosophy. The salesperson discovers what is valuable to the buyer and then seeks ways to increase the value of his offering. Value-added selling also means taking the initiative to proactively seek ways to increase the value of your company, product, and yourself to the buyer. The value-added salesperson has two objectives. First, he wants to satisfy the buyer's needs and then some! Second, he wants to do this in a way that is profitable for his organization. A value-oriented philosophy then serves as the catalyst for the value-added sales approach.

In the value-added sale, there are three distinct phases. Phase one is the planning phase. This is where you analyze all of the variables that influence the buyer's decision and then set your objectives. This is sometimes referred to as the precall phase: analyzing decision variables, making appointments, setting objectives, etc. Phase two is the implementation phase. This is where you make the sales call. You interview the buyer thoroughly to determine his needs and then tailor your presentation of features and benefits to address his needs specifically. The implementation phase can be one or several calls. The third phase of the value-added sale is the follow-up phase. This is where you assure buyer satisfaction, assuage buyer remorse, and review your calling efforts.

The primary task for the value-added salesperson is to define value in the buyer's terms. Study his needs and speculate how your product offers him greater value. Share your insights with him. It's his objective awareness of his needs, coupled with a promise of greater value, that creates a sense of urgency to act. Seek ways to add more value and then offer these value-oriented solutions to the buyer.

ARE YOU CUTTING YOUR PRICES OR YOUR THROAT?

So you think it makes sense to cut your prices to sell more products? When deciding whether to cut your prices, make sure you're not cutting your throat. Let's see how prudent your decision is.

Let's first examine the psychological impact of price slashing. How do existing customers perceive your price-cutting strategy? They could interpret this as an admission that your prices were too high all along. You've been gouging them! They may resent it rather than welcome it with open arms. Your strategy backfired! It may even create speculation that additional price cuts are imminent. This causes a wait-and-see attitude in the marketplace: "Let's wait and see if the prices will go even lower than they are now!" Remember calculators, video recorders, and car phones?

By lowering your prices, you're setting a dangerous precedent. You're telling the buyer that lower prices are possible. If he holds out long enough, perhaps he'll get an even better deal. This is the concept under which most auto buyers operate. Who pays full sticker price for a car? Nobody. The reason is they don't have to. The precedent has been set.

Cutting your prices could also give the impression that your company, personnel, and products are not as good as the competition's. You're positioning yourself as number two, three, or four. You're telling the buyer inadvertently that you're not as creative as the competition and your only defense is a better price: "Our strongest advantage is our price!" What's the impact of this on employees? Workers start believing that your quality is lower than the competition. They are less motivated to produce high quality products. You've created a self-fulfilling prophecy that has further diminished your position in the marketplace.

How does price-cutting influence you as a salesperson?

Your confidence level in your company and product begins to wane. How do you think you would fare in a competitive sales situation where quality was the major criterion? Is it possible that you've psyched yourself out to the point where you feel noncompetitive? If so, the buyer knows it. Does lowering your prices really make sense? How does price-cutting affect your motivation as a salesperson? Do you feel as excited about servicing this customer when he gets bargain basement pricing? Have you ever taken a piece of business and then regretted it afterward? Maybe you even resented the customer because you felt that you got the short end of the deal.

Consider the more pragmatic implications of lowering your prices. Your profit margins erode. Eroding profit margins generally mean there is less money for things like research and development, bonus programs, quality control, administrative support, etc. When you begin shaving resources vis-à-vis reduced profit margins, your long-term competitiveness is damaged severely. You create a situation where you will be less competitive in the future. Consequently, you'll need to cut your prices again to stay in the game. How long can that go on before you go out of business?

For years people have justified cutting their prices because they could make it up with increased volume. If you're selling at $0.97 on the dollar, do you really feel you'll make it up in volume? The one thing they failed to tell you in your introductory economics course is that your company may not be able to handle the extra volume needed to compensate for the reduced profit margin. Extra volume could mean hiring more people and purchasing additional equipment to handle the volume. More personnel and equipment lower the already suffering profit margins. You've created a chain reaction. Lower prices means more volume means greater resources means lower margins means greater volume means even greater demands for resources, ad infinitum. Or it could end up somewhere short of infinity: bankruptcy court!

If you're still unconvinced that lowering your prices can have undesirable consequences, consider this: how much more do you need to sell to compensate for the loss in your gross margins? Here's a hypothetical example:

	A Sell at List	B Discount 15%	C Increase Needed
Sales Volume	500,000	425,000	610,000
Direct Costs	250,000	250,000	360,000
	(50%)	(59%)	(59%)
Gross Profit	250,000	175,000	250,000
	(50%)	(41%)	(41%)
Variable Expense	70,000	70,000	70,000
	(14%)	(16.4%)	(11%)
Fixed Expense	150,000	150,000	150,000
	(30%)	(32.2%)	(25%)
Net Profit	30,000	(45,000)	30,000
	(6%)		(5%)

In Example A you're selling at your normal list price. Your gross profit is 50 percent, and you're earning 6 percent net profit. In Example B you've cut your selling price by 15 percent to be more competitive. After all, a 15 percent discount when you're earning 50 percent to begin with isn't that much, is it? Notice that your direct costs in B (how much the products cost you) haven't changed. Only the selling price changes, which reduces your gross profit in B. Your fixed and variable costs of doing business have not changed. But look at the bottom line. You're in the hole for $45,000!

Example C illustrates the additional sales volume needed just to make sure your bottom line stays at $30,000. If you compute the ratios, you'll discover that you need to increase your sales volume to $610,000 at a 15 percent discount just to contribute $30,000 to the bottom line. This is a whopping 43 percent increase in sales just to contribute the same amount of money to your company's bottom line. Can you sell this additional volume? Do you want to have to sell this additional volume? Probably not!

This example demonstrates the impact that discounting has on your profitability. Be cognizant of this impact. Selling greater volume can be misleading. There are two fundamental questions you must ask yourself before cutting your prices. The first is "What is your company's goal: large volume or profitability?" The second is "Do you want every order or every opportunity?" There is some business out there you don't want. Define these parameters in advance, and make a prudent business decision.

Before you decide to discount, try this exercise. Make two lists on a piece of paper. Under the heading *Impact on Us*, list all the implications for your company when you cut the price. Itemize how it adversely affects your organization. Under the heading *Impact on the Customer*, list all the implications for your customer when you cut prices. Point out the negative consequences the customer experiences. You should easily come up with a list of at least a dozen ideas. These ideas are the seeds of your responses to the customer's request for a better deal. Go through your list of consequences with the customer and point out the disadvantages of lowering the price.

It's my position that you already know the answers to price objections. It's more a matter of your presenting these ideas in a cohesive fashion.

FUN FACTS REGARDING PRICE

Based on my research and experience, I've compiled a list of facts that are important considerations relative to the price issue. Use these to make better decisions.

- In the absence of all other information, brand name is still the best indicator for quality. This is the latest finding in a market research study in which consumers rank different variables. The implication is that if you sell brand name items, buyers perceive greater value in your product vis-à-vis quality.

- Market leaders can easily charge more than the competition. If your prices are about 7 percent above industry average and you market well, you'll have no trouble maintaining your share of the pie.

- If you charge more, people perceive greater value. Conversely, there is a reverse trend toward lower-priced goods. If your products are too cheap, people don't want them. They assume that something must be wrong with them.

- Buyers are more price sensitive for the necessities in life than the niceties. If it's a frillish item, buyers don't balk. On the other hand, when buying commodities they're more concerned with price. After all, when was the last time you heard someone complain about the price of a new Mercedes?

- Fewer than one in five is a true price shopper.

- Some price shoppers are actually compulsive personalities, and getting a bargain is actually more important to them than the price.

- Some people are situational price shoppers. They may be dealing with limited funds for a given project, and this motivates them to shop price. Under different circumstances, this person may not even challenge your price.

- I've trained many salespeople from companies that are the least expensive in their industry. These people usually ask me, "Tom, how do I sell against greater value? What can I do to compete with a company that offers better service and quality?" Isn't it ironic that they want to know how to compete with you, the value-added salesperson, while you want to know how to sell against price?

You could summarize most of these facts by saying that the greater perceived value you bring to the sale, the fewer price objections you encounter. Invest your selling time well. Pursue ways to add value instead of cutting prices.

MYTHS OF VALUE-ADDED SELLING

I've heard some interesting comments about value-added selling from people whom I've trained. Some of them believe in any one or more of these erroneous myths about value-added selling. Some believe that value-added selling applies to only very complex technical sales with lengthy sales cycles. Wrong! Some of the most successful stories we've witnessed have come from organizations that sell commodity products or companies that distribute exactly the same product as six other companies in their area. These companies have discovered ways to differentiate their "bundled package."

Another myth is that value-added selling applies only to the product. Wrong! These people haven't recognized the importance of the vendor who brings the product to market or the salesperson who acts as the liaison between the customer and the vendor. It's a conservative estimate that the vendor and the salesperson count at least as much as the product.

Closely related to this myth is the belief that only management or product managers can design and deliver added value for the customer. Wrong! Again, the salesperson can shape the value of his offering with his contribution.

Another myth is that just because everyone offers a special feature or benefit, it's not worth mentioning. Wrong! Just because everyone else does it does not make a particular feature less important. Also, I would not assume that just because the competition has it, they flaunt it.

I came to this conclusion after having just completed a cycle of training in the computer industry. You would think that in an industry where companies have access to the latest in desktop publishing and laser printers their presentations and proposals would reflect this. I was astonished when I surveyed these companies to see how many actually failed to put their best foot forward during the sales process. Many of them used dot-matrix printers which look OK but certainly don't project the image of a laser. And some of these companies even used a standard typewriter for their proposals! They didn't use all of the resources available to them.

By correcting these myths, we are setting ourselves on a course for sales success. If we apply the principles of value-added selling and follow the rules, this journey is almost complete.

RULES OF VALUE-ADDED SELLING

Understanding these fundamental principles can make your value-added selling efforts easier and more effective.

- Customer satisfaction is a function of the customer's expectations relative to your performance as a vendor. If you promise a lot and deliver more, you have satisfied customers who will likely pay more to buy from your company. If you promise a lot and deliver less, you have customer dissatisfaction. Customers will likely complain about price in addition to your service problems.
- You don't want every order—you want every opportunity. There is some business out there you don't want. The low-profit, high-aggravation factor business is that which you want your competition to have. But you would at least like the opportunity to turn it away.
- You can't make a good deal with a bad guy. If the person with whom you're dealing is unscrupulous, don't expect fair treatment. If it's feasible, this may be a piece of business you want the competition to have.
- No product is overpriced unless it's underdesired. If you get a price objection, it's generally because you haven't convinced the buyer sufficiently of the value of your offering.
- Not all customers are value-added targets. All customers deserve the courtesy of a value-added mindset, but it's unproductive to deliver value-added services

to all customers. On some it would be wasted. The intensity of value-added sales effort is such that its recipients must be carefully selected.

- The stronger the relationship between the buyer and seller, the less important the role price plays. When people trust each other and want to do business, they generally figure a way to make it happen. I recently attended a purchasing seminar and was impressed by the comments I heard from purchasing agents. Buyers are just as concerned about the relationship as salespeople; and with both parties that concerned, good things will happen.

Selling value results in a double win. The customer feels good because he's been treated fairly. We feel good because we made a sale and a friend. Understanding these rules can help us engineer the value-added sale. Following these rules can help us achieve our goals.

CHAPTER SUMMARY

Value is like beauty: it's in the eye of the beholder. What is valuable to you is not necessarily valuable to me. Your task is to determine how the buyer defines value because those terms dictate how to present your product. Remember that nothing is overpriced unless it is underdesired by the other person.

Lowering your prices may be a good strategy once you consider the impact of your action. All of us meet price objections in one way or another. We either cut our prices or increase the value of our products and services. Price cutting is only one option.

If price were the only thing your buyers purchased, why would your company need you? Couldn't your organization send out weekly or monthly price bulletins and accomplish the same thing? In fact, your company could lower the selling price by eliminating your salary, bonus, and expenses and pass that savings along to the customer. That's a scary thought for most salespeople, but it brings up a relevant issue. In sales, we're paid to sell as profitably as we can for our companies. That's our mission, and that's what this book is all about.

2
Planning

Your first major step in selling value versus price is in the planning stage of the sale. Here, you lay the groundwork for commanding a higher price. Your preparation for the sales call determines your success on the sales call.

Planning carries with it a host of benefits. When you plan, you feel more confident. You're able to answer most questions the buyer throws your way. Planning helps you control the sales call because you know what you want to happen at each step along the way. When you prepare for the call, you create a more professional image, and the buyer shares your confidence. Consequently, he's willing to pay a little more because of it. Preparation avoids surprises. It's tough to get blindsided when you're well prepared. Simply stated, preparation coupled with knowledge is power. And when you sell value rather than price, you need all of the power you can get.

In this chapter, I have a very simple objective: I want to show you how to prepare yourself for making the value-added sales call.

Specifically, we'll focus on two issues. The first is the value-added planning model. It's a problem-solving model designed to help you view the situation in such a way that you are able to bring additional value to the sale. Simply, it shows you how to understand value from your customer's perspective. It builds your knowledge base and helps you customize your sales strategy.

Second, we'll examine call objectives and how, by setting these objectives, you increase the likelihood of your success. When you approach the customer in an organized rather than agonized manner, you control the sale. You're prepared and it shows. When you're in control and prepared, you're more confident. And when you're more confident, you close more deals.

In short, planning equips you with self-confidence and knowledge. When you plan, you think strategically. When you think strategically, you sell value, not price.

VALUE-ADDED PLANNING MODEL

The value-added planning model is a five-step problem-solving, brainstorming, strategic analysis, and planning process that enables you to customize a sales approach for a given account. It's a thorough model for determining how to sell value to your customer. By using it, you're able to differentiate your company, your solution, and yourself from the competition. In short, it helps you and your customer make better business decisions.

Step One: Problem Definition

In this step, you want to gather all information about the account that is relevant to the situation. This includes information about your customer's competition. Try to piece together the scenario for why the customer is applying pressure for a better price. Include all facts that have a bearing on the situation: market facts, your competitors, driving forces behind the customer's needs, etc.

List these facts on a sheet of paper or planning flip chart and sort through them for relevance. Begin with two categories: relevant and not relevant. Scratch through the not relevant. Then rank the relevant facts in order of priority. Ask yourself, "What's most important of these relevant facts?"

If you're working with someone else on this account, discuss the available information. If you're working alone, discuss it with your boss or a peer whose opinion you value. Try to get a clear understanding of the problem and write a concise description of it. This ensures that you fully understand it.

Step Two: Vision Clarification

Now you want to set objectives for this account. Think long- and short-term. If you set objectives with a timetable for their completion, there's a much greater likelihood of your achieving these goals. Salespeople who are goal-directed are more productive. They sell more, and they sell more profitably.

Begin with an overall mission statement for the account. This is what you want to happen in the long haul with them. It's what you're working toward. A mission statement might include things like maximum account control, thorough account penetration, sustained profitability, the quality standard, etc. Here's a sample account mission statement:

> Our mission for this account is to gain maximum control for the products we sell this customer and to increase our profitability on these items while maintaining a significant competitive advantage.

As you can see, this isn't very specific but it does set the tone for your sales efforts. It provides you with direction. Your specific account goals that tend to have a shorter time frame must support this account mission statement. Shorter-term specific goals include things like target sales volume, gross profit objectives, type of products to be emphasized, etc.

Your job becomes infinitely easier when you have a sense of purpose or direction. You tend to stay on course and achieve your desired results much more quickly. Setting goals for your account will help you sell added value to your customers.

Step Three: Needs Survey

Once you have set the tone for your sales efforts by clarifying your vision and by reviewing all critical data in the problem definition, you may discover that there is still some information you need. It could be that there are a couple of missing pieces you still need to collect from the customer.

Make a list of this information and go to the appropriate source. If it's the customer, make a list of the questions you need answered. This fills in the blanks from Step One. You may also discover that there are no blanks. There is no need to probe further. You already have enough information to move ahead. In that case, skip Step Three. It's optional. It's an extra step that's designed to help you get anything else you need prior to your brainstorming.

Step Four: Study Phase

The purpose of this step is to consolidate all of the information you've collected with the information you already had. After doing this, you want to brainstorm for ideas or ways in which you can add value to the sale for the customer. It's also a decision phase in which you consider the implications of action versus inertia. Then select your strategy.

Should we or shouldn't we? This is the magic question we must ask prior to suggesting any value-added ideas to the customer. Do we really want to significantly invest our resources in this account? Can we win the wait-and-see game? Can we afford to do nothing? Or is the payoff for doing something significant enough to move ahead? Does the return justify the investment? If you determine that action is better than inertia, look for possible ways to add value to the sale. The following model will help you in your search.

Brainstorming for value-added ideas is an exciting process. Generally, it involves two steps. The first is to quantify your ideas, and the second is to qualify your ideas. In quantifying, you conceive of as many ideas as possible. Go for quantity initially. Your immediate objective is to get many ideas on the table.

To assist you in this search for ideas ask yourself the question, "What can we do to make the customer's life easier?" At this point, write down everything that comes to mind. Something that could help you is to focus on specific critical impact areas in the customer's business. These areas include marketing, warehousing, shipping, receiving, training, manufacturing, service, ordering, etc. Again, ask yourself questions in these areas. For example:

- "What can we do to make it easier for our customers to order?"
- "How can we help our customers better market their products?"
- "What can we do to help our customers familiarize themselves more quickly with our equipment?"

For each of these questions and others you ask, write down any answer you give. Even if it seems like a strange idea, it could represent the seed of a more powerful idea. Don't worry about the quality of these ideas yet. Simply go for numbers.

Once you have amassed a list of options, select the best ones by using certain criteria. For example, you might qualify the list with these:

- ease of implementation
- expense
- time investment
- customer perception of value
- proven usage history

There may even be some additional criteria that you want to use. The objective is to build a list of feasible and productive value-added extras that will help your company gain or maintain a competitive advantage. Your goal is to become so valuable that the customer can't afford to do business without you.

Step Five: Implementation

This step involves several things. First, it means preparing your organization to deliver the value-added services. Discuss the strategy and reasons with all those people who will be actively involved. Get their commitment through involvement. Ensure that everyone connected with the strategy understands his or her role. Customer satisfaction depends on performance of this strategy. Remember, perception plays a major role in your winning the business, but it is the performance of greater value that enables you to maintain the business.

Prepare the customer for the extras he'll receive. Ensure that his expectations are consistent with what you've promised. There's only one thing worse than promising more than you can deliver. It's called the "sin of omission." This is when you let the customer believe that something will happen when you know that it won't. You have not overtly lied, but you left the customer with the expectation that something would happen and it didn't. In this case, you still have a dissatisfied customer because your performance didn't live up to the customer's expectations. Remember, promise a lot and deliver more! If this is your policy, you'll always have satisfied customers.

When preparing your customers, they must fully understand that which is expected from them. If they play a major role in the value-added extra you're delivering, be sure that they know what to do and when to do it. It's disappointing to go the extra mile and then lose it because of a breakdown on the customer's end.

Once the value-added extras are in place and working, it's

prudent to check on yourself to determine whether your ideas are performing their original purpose. Are you getting the full value-added impact from them? Does the customer fully appreciate what you've done? Have these value-added extras differentiated your company the way you wanted them to do? What changes could you make to maximize your impact? Could you use these ideas somewhere else?

Planning to sell added value is an important step in delivering the extras. Thorough planning increases your odds for successful implementation. I've found that a major reason salespeople do not sell added value is that they don't understand it. This model was designed to help you understand, plan, and implement the value-added philosophy.

CALL PREPARATION

As the name implies, this is where you collect your thoughts and organize your sales strategy prior to making the call. The more time spent collecting and organizing your thoughts before the call, the greater the likelihood you'll sell your ideas. Call preparation entails setting call objectives and planning how you'll achieve these objectives.

Call Objectives

There are two magic questions you must ask yourself prior to making the sales call. These two questions encourage you to think incisively about your goals for this call. Answer these questions and you'll sell more because you'll be better prepared.

"What Do I Want to Accomplish on This Call?"

The answer to this is your call objective. There are really seven reasons why you would call on a customer. Understanding which one applies to a given call helps you plan your sales strategy.

Reason #1: Sell a product—This is only one of seven reasons why you would make a sales call, but it's an important one.

Reason #2: Gather information—With this call objective, you want to gather facts. You may want to collect information about a variety of topics: the marketplace, your competition, your company's performance-to-expectations level, or you may want to gather information regarding the buyer's world.

Reason #3: Give information—Your purpose in giving information is to become the single greatest information resource the buyer has. You want to be his information pulse. Give information in these areas: the market, his competition (provided you're not selling to his competition), information regarding his customers, general business information that makes him a better businessperson. For example, you could provide your buyer with a classic article on inventory control that could help him save enough money in one area to spend for your products in another area. Educating your customer builds loyalty that can't be bought for a cheaper price.

Reason #4: Plant seeds—When you plant seeds you're making the buyer aware that you have something "in the works" for the future. Your purpose is to cultivate the soil by creating a needs awareness and flirting with a potential solution.

Reason #5: Assure satisfaction—Another reason to call on a customer is to assure he's satisfied with what you've sold him. Because of your commitment as a value-oriented salesperson, you have an obligation to follow up with your customers. There are two times when you want to do this. First, contact your customer between commitment and delivery to assuage buyer remorse. Second, follow up after delivery to ensure that the buyer has received his money's worth and that the product is operating correctly.

Reason #6: Handle complaints—Unfortunately, many of us have had to make sales calls for the express purpose of handling customer complaints. This is one call objective you hope not to use very often. When it occurs, use these ideas. Have a list of concessions you can make to appease the other person. Be prepared to listen nonjudgmentally and avoid saying anything that indicates defensiveness. Empathize and focus on solutions. Worry about fixing the problem instead of fixing the blame. Use this as an opportunity to demonstrate service and class.

Reason #7: Gain referrals—What better time is there for you to actively seek a referral than when you're with a satisfied customer? On each and every sales call, ask for the name of someone who could benefit from your products or services. At the very least this should be your secondary call objective.

"What Do I Want the Customer to Do at the End of This Call?"

This second question is your customer-action objective. It's the thing you want your customer to do as you finish the call. Ironically, it's the question most salespeople fail to ask themselves. If you answer this question before making the call, you'll know how to ask for action at the end of the call. Here are some ideas for customer-action objectives:

- The prospect gives you the name of a referral.
- The prospect agrees to take your ideas to a committee.
- The prospect arranges for a meeting with other decision makers.
- The prospect gives you a purchase order number.
- The prospect agrees to try a sample.

The list is endless, but you'll notice each of these suggestions has a common denominator: action! We're stressing that action which we expect the customer to take at the end of the call. Closing is a lot easier when we know what it is that we want the customer to do.

By giving advance thought to what you want to achieve

on your sales call, you are more likely to reach your goals. It builds your confidence and resilience. It prepares you for the best and the worst. That's what I call "prepared spontaneity."

Call Planning Guide

The last step in preparing for your sales call is completing your call planning guide. This is your road map to successful selling. Salespeople who use this guide speak of the tremendous wave of self-confidence shrouding them while filling it out. You can use the format that appears below or develop your own, but be sure to include the key elements from this diagram.

Call Planning Guide

Account: _____

Person: _____

My Call Objective: _____

Customer-Action Objective: _____

Sales Aids Needed: _____

Customer's Needs/Problems: _____

Opening Statement: _____

_____

Needs Analysis Questions: _____

_____

_____

_____

Benefits to Stress: _____

_____

_____

Anticipated Objections and Responses: _____

_____

_____

_____

Closing Strategy: _____

_____

From the diagram, it's obvious that this doesn't need to be a lengthy process. It should take a maximum of twenty minutes to complete this. By filling out this guide, you control as many of the details as you can. This increases your motivation to make the call and your enthusiasm while you're on the call. Call preparation, which includes setting objectives, preparing value-analysis examples, and filling out a call planning guide, puts you in the catbird's seat for selling value.

CHAPTER SUMMARY

In this chapter, we explored four major areas that help you plan to sell value rather than price. As you might have gathered by now, selling value is a real commitment, and that's why the rewards are so great. Once you've defined your value-oriented market and performed a strategic value analysis, you can use that information to create significant barriers in your product, company, and selling style. Your next step is to plan your call. Prepare yourself for the value-added sales call. More importantly, prepare yourself for the success you'll enjoy.

3
The Opening Stage

This is the very first step in your face-to-face meeting with the prospect. It could be the initial cold call or the one-hundredth time you've called on this buyer. Your objective is simple. You want to gain early control of the conversation and set a positive tone for the remainder of the call.

The opening stage has three critical elements: introductions, stating the purpose of your call, and asking permission to probe.

INTRODUCTIONS

As you open the call, exchange the customary amenities. Introduce yourself, shake hands, and give a brief overview statement about your company. If you've met with this person before, this stage will be shorter than on your initial call. Avoid giving too much information about your company at this point. Remember that your objective is to open the call and set a positive tone.

Keep your introductions to a few sentences. For example: "Good morning, Mr. Buyer. My name is Frank Mahoney with Jason Engines. I'm pleased to finally meet you in person. As I mentioned on the phone, Jason supplies the aviation industry with high-performance replacement parts for engines."

Notice that I kept the introductions brief. There's a tendency for salespeople to want to overstay their welcome in the opening stage. Many feel it's a way to build rapport. Rapport is important, and you'll learn in the next chapter how to build it by asking questions in the needs-analysis stage.

STATE THE PURPOSE OF YOUR CALL

When you tell the buyer why you're there, state a benefit for him or his company. Your purpose in calling on this buyer is to help him in some way: save money or time, find a safer way to do something, offer convenience, and so on. Simply tell him you're there to help. Generally, this begins with: "My reason for calling on you is . . ." or "The reason I'm here today is. . . ."

State your benefit after this lead-in phrase. For example: "The reason I wanted to meet with you today is to show you how Jason can offer you a cost-efficient way to replace broken parts on your engines." When you combine this with the introductory statement we used in the last section, it becomes conversational magic.

ASK PERMISSION TO PROBE

This is your transition to the needs-analysis stage. With this bridge, you ask the buyer for his permission to ask questions. We do this for several reasons. First, it's polite. If you're going to ask several questions in the needs analysis, it's common courtesy to alert the other person to see if he has any reservations about this. Second, your bridge is a built-in reminder of what you will do next: ask questions.

Third, when the buyer says, "Fine, go ahead and ask away," he's made a strong commitment to answering your questions. This is the most important reason for you to bridge—to get his commitment to answering your questions. Here's how you do it: "To determine how we can do this, would you mind if I start with a few questions?"

Wait for his commitment and then proceed with the needs-analysis stage. When you put all three of these pieces together, your opening stage flows smoothly. For example:

> Good morning, Mr. Buyer. My name is Frank Mahoney with Jason Engines. I'm pleased to finally meet you in person. As I mentioned on the phone, Jason supplies aviation companies with high-performance replacement parts for engines.
>
> The reason I wanted to meet with you today is to show you how Jason can offer you a cost-efficient way to replace parts on your engines.
>
> To determine how we can do this, would you mind if I start with a few questions?

When designing your opening comments, use your own language. Don't get hung up on the words I used in my examples. Make it sound like you talking. Make it planned—not canned.

CHAPTER SUMMARY

The opening stage of the sale is brief. You should spend less than a minute opening the call. Remember that your purpose is to gain quick conversational control and to set a positive tone for the call. Use the three elements described in this chapter to develop a strong opening stage: make introductions, state the purpose of your call, and ask permission to probe.

At the end of Chapter Six is an outline to show you how to execute the value-added sales call from the opening stage to the commitment stage.

4
The Needs-Analysis Stage

Imagine that you're in your doctor's office. He's describing a new medication for diabetes patients—extolling the virtues of this revolutionary drug. It's readily available and offers patients an annual savings of 40 percent over standard insulin. Obviously, your doctor is excited about this new product. He writes a prescription for you.

You're confused, because you're there for a flu shot. Beyond that, you don't even have diabetes! The doctor prescribed without examining your symptoms.

How many times have you done this to your buyer? Many salespeople make calls detailing their product assuming that the buyer needs it and knows he needs it. It's an assumption you cannot make. If you want to sell effectively, you must first analyze the buyer's needs thoroughly.

The needs-analysis stage is a communicative fact-finding mission—an exploration into the buyer's needs, wants, and desires. It's even more than that: it's an in-depth examination and evaluation of all those variables that potentially could influence the buying decision. You gather objective data and the buyer's subjective perceptions regarding these needs. It is the most important phase of the sale because it enables you to correctly prescribe the right solution for the buyer's problems.

By thoroughly analyzing the buyer's needs, you help him objectively understand his needs. It's this objective awareness that raises his constructive "pain level" with the status quo. Our strategic questioning is the catalyst to his dissatisfaction with his current way of *attempting* to meet his needs. This catalyst incites action to change.

Probing for buyer needs highlights the nonprice variables that affect the buying decision. Getting the prospect to elaborate on the importance of these nonprice variables mitigates the role of price in the buying decision.

Early management studies tell us that involvement in the change process builds commitment and lowers resistance to new ideas. Involving the prospect through questioning breaks down his resistance to change and builds commitment. When you couple an objective awareness of one's situation with this active involvement, the motivation to change comes from within the individual. The prospect wants to change, which makes your job easier.

After getting the buyer involved, raising his objective-awareness level, and creating an internal motivation to change, the net result is simple: the buyer is more eager to buy than you are to sell. What does that do to your closing ratio? Do you think price plays a major role in the buying decision if the buyer's desire to own your product is greater than your desire to sell? No way! Price is then relegated to the position it richly deserves: only one of many buying criteria rather than the main reason someone buys a product.

Consider this icing on the cake. When you probe, you're telegraphing strong messages to your prospect. You're saying, "I care enough to listen—enough to invest part of my life to hear your problems." This builds trust and rapport. It also differentiates you from all other salespeople who call on that buyer and deliver canned presentations. You're recording a strong message on the tape inside the buyer's head.

The prospect says to himself, "This person cares enough to listen to my concerns. He knows my problems and is committed to a viable solution for them. He's different from most other salespeople who've called on me. I want to do business with him because I trust him."

The premise is simple. If two people want to do business with each other because of trust and rapport, the details (like price) rarely block the sale. If the buyer trusts you and feels comfortable with you because of your genuine concern, price doesn't preclude your doing business. If you develop this rapport with the prospect, price weighs less in the buying decision.

By performing the needs analysis, you communicate, "It's OK to pay a little more for the value we offer. We understand your problems and share your concerns. We're committed to finding a solution that makes sense for you."

A failure to perform a needs analysis leaves few options. You deliver a canned presentation because you're unaware of all the mediating variables that diminish the importance of price. You fail to build the trust and rapport needed for the value-added sales call.

MECHANICS OF QUESTIONING

The first step in developing a needs analysis is a thorough understanding of the mechanics of asking questions. You must know how to construct questions that give you the information you desire. When designing your questions, consider these three areas: length of response, intent, and bias.

Length of Response

Your first consideration is how lengthy a response you want and need.

An open-ended question prompts the respondent to elaborate or expound. It requires more than just a few words—a lengthy response. The advantage of this is that the buyer volunteers additional information and explains his position more thoroughly. It builds commitment because of active prospect involvement and avoids the interrogation effect. A disadvantage of an open-ended question is that it is time-consuming, and you may lose some conversational control.

Typically, open-ended questions begin with "why, how, what, tell me about, . . ." or any other word or phrase designed to gain active participation. A facial expression could be construed as an open-ended question if it encourages the other person to respond freely. Here are some examples of open-ended questions:

- Why do you feel that way?
- What are your main concerns in buying?
- Tell me about your business.
- How do you feel about dealing with more than one supplier?
- Why is price such an important variable in your decision process?

A closed-ended question elicits a short response—generally, one or two words. You intentionally limit the response length. The closed-ended question offers two advantages: it gives you greater conversational control and it is more time-efficient. The primary disadvantage is that the respondent isn't prompted to offer unsolicited information. Also, the buyer may feel grilled and interrogated if too many closed-ended questions are used consecutively.

Generally, closed-ended questions begin with "when, who, which, where, how many, how much, do you, are you, will you," etc. Notice that all of these examples have one thing in common: they evoke a shorter response.

- How often do you order these items?
- Which of these do you prefer?

- When do you place orders?
- Have you had problems getting these from your current supplier?

You can get the same information from the respondent by asking either an open-ended or a closed-ended question. For example:

(Open)   What role does price play in your buying decision?

(Closed) Is price an important variable in your buying decision?

The open-ended question encourages a lengthier response. An advantage of this is that the prospect might tell you why price is so important. Any information you want can be submitted to this exercise and asked in either way. Ideally, you should ask all open-ended questions. Realistically, you may need to ask a few closed-ended questions to regain control or confirm what was told you in a lengthy response. For example:

    (Open) What are your major concerns in purchasing?

(Lengthy response)

    (Closed) Then price and delivery are your two major concerns?

Use this rule of thumb to encourage the buyer to respond freely. Ask four times as many open-ended questions as you do closed-ended questions. For every five questions you ask, four should be open-ended and only one closed-ended. If the conversation drifts out on a tangent, ask a closed-ended question to regain quick control.

People often ask me in seminars, "How do I get the silent type to open up?" My recommendation is to examine the nature of the questions you ask. You probably ask too many closed-ended questions that inhibit buyer participation.

Keep your questions open-ended to encourage full participation of both parties.

Intent

The second area to consider in designing questions is your intent. How obvious do you want to be with your questions? How blunt and straightforward can you afford to be?

A direct question is blunt, straightforward, and to the point. There is no doubt what you're asking. It's obvious. An advantage to this approach is that there is no confusion about the information you want. It may even be more time-efficient. A strong disadvantage to the direct question is that it's generally offensive and threatening. Look at these examples.

- Do you have the authority to make this decision?
- Is price important to you?
- Why do you buy from that supplier?

There is a strong element of risk in these questions because they are so blunt. In most cases, it is prudent to soften these questions and minimize the perceived threat. Do this with an indirect question.

An indirect question veils your intent. It's oblique and circuitous. It's a roundabout way of getting the same information. One advantage is that it's easier to answer since it's not as threatening. Because it is a low-risk question, you're more likely to get a response. The indirect question also encourages the other person to volunteer additional information. A disadvantage is that it may not be as time-efficient because what you're asking isn't as obvious. Here are some examples:

- How does your purchasing procedure work?
- What things are important to you in making your buying decision?
- Do you have more than one supplier?

Notice that these parallel the direct question examples. In the first example, I give the prospect an opportunity to save face because I don't question his buying authority. Rather, I ask how the buying process works in general. It offers him a chance to volunteer that he is or is not the decision maker. I get my information in a nonthreatening manner.

In the second example, I don't call attention to the price issue. Rather, I ask about *all* things that are important in this decision. It raises the prospect's awareness that there are considerations other than price. I don't assume price is the only criterion. If price is important, I still find out with his answer.

With the third question, I ask how many suppliers he has. My intent is to get him talking about all of his suppliers. This way I can discover what I really want to know: why he buys from a given supplier. It's an oblique way of getting the information, but the buyer may be more receptive to indirect questions. Here is another example of how to change a direct question into an indirect question.

(Direct)	Do you believe in gun control?
(Indirect)	How do you think most people feel about gun control?

I made this indirect by asking about everyone's opinions, not just yours. Indirectly, your response suggests your feelings, and this tells me what I want to know.

The best time to use an indirect question is when you feel the nature of the question is risky enough to warrant some caution. Broach the topic indirectly to get your information. If you perceive less risk, ask the question more directly.

Window Exercise

You can combine intent with length of response and ask for the same information four ways. Imagine the flexibility this gives you! Here are some examples:

	Open	**Closed**
Direct	1. Tell me about your involvement in the buying decision. 2. What role does price play in your final decision to buy?	1. Do you have the authority to make this decision? 2. Is price your main concern?
Indirect	1. How are these buying decisions normally made? 2. What things are important when you make your buying decision?	1. Is there a standard way of making these buying decisions? 2. Do you have something that is most important when making your buying decision?

This exercise builds your flexibility in asking questions. You minimize risk and reduce the perceived threat by moving from direct-closed to indirect-open.

	Open	**Closed**
Direct	1 Moderate Risk	2 Greatest Risk
Indirect	3 Least Risk	4 Lower Risk

Make a list of all the questions you'd love to ask your buyer if you were given a green light. Select the most threatening, and use the window exercise to soften it. Move from quadrant two to quadrant three. Watch the reaction of your prospect when you ask these indirect-open questions. He'll volunteer information beyond your wildest dreams. By making these low-risk, nonthreatening questions, you make it easier for the respondent to answer.

Bias

This is the third area to consider when designing your questions. Do you want an objective, factually based response, or do you want a mirrored echo of what you ask? Do you want the prospect to speak freely or just give you responses reflecting agreement with your assumptions? Do you want to ask questions that encourage dialogue, or do you want to ask questions that lead the other person?

Remember, your objective at this phase of the sale is to engage the buyer, open him up, and receive bountiful information. Leading questions discourage this give-and-take environment.

A neutral question offers no suggestion of what the response should be. It doesn't lead the other person. Consequently, he doesn't feel threatened. On the other hand, a leading question suggests the answer you desire. It leaves little room for the respondent to volunteer his opinions.

(Neutral)	Is price important?
(Leading)	Price is important, isn't it?
(Neutral)	Are you the decision maker?
(Leading)	You're the decision maker, aren't you?

A leading question makes buyers feel defensive because it forces a response. How do you feel when someone uses leading or biased questions on you? If you're like most people, you resent being told what to think and say. You feel cornered, manipulated, and controlled, none of which is conducive to rapport-building or gaining objective information.

Sales trainers who teach the use of leading questions in

this phase of the sale are "misleading" you. They're encouraging you to use techniques on others that you resent people using on you. There is an inconsistency here. Salespeople don't use skills that are philosophically incongruent with their own value structures. Your caveat is to avoid bias in your questions during the needs analysis. Remember, your objective is to gather facts—not elicit canned responses.

STRATEGIC QUESTIONING AREAS

It's as important for you to know in which areas to ask questions as it is for you to know how to ask questions. The purpose of this section is to show you how to arrange your questions. Asking your questions in this order capitalizes on the logic of the needs analysis. Divide your questions into these three categories: situational, competitive, and projective questions.

Situational Questions

These extract information about the customer's world: his goals, wants, needs, decision process, etc. The buyer gives you vital information regarding all of those variables that influence his buying decision. Subdivide your situational questions into these two groups: general business and specific need.

General business questions are global, broad-based, non-threatening types of questions that spark the conversation and provide a useful backdrop. General business questions focus on these things about the buyer's world: his market, his customer, his company, his competition, and himself. Under each of these five areas are several questions you could ask. Here are some examples of each.

(Market)   Tell me about your marketplace.
(Market)   What trends do you see in your market?

(Customer)	Who are your customers?
(Customer)	What do your customers look for when they come to you?
(Company)	How does your decision process work?
(Company)	How long has your company been in this market?
(Competition)	Who are your competitors?
(Competition)	What advantages do you have over them?
(Himself)	How long have you been with the company?
(Himself)	How does this decision affect you personally?

Notice that these questions are nonthreatening and good conversation starters. You may not need to ask as many as I have listed here, but at the very least you would want to ask, "Tell me about your business."

"Specific need" is the second group of situational questions. Here you ask for the prospect's needs, wants, requirements, and expectations from a supplier and a product. Get the necessary facts to determine whether your company and product are a good match for his needs. Ask questions about specifications and delivery dates. Determine budget limitations. Find out what quality he needs.

(Company)	What are you looking for in a supplier?
(Company)	What kind of technical support do you need on this project?
(Product)	What delivery and availability does your project require?
(Product)	Tell me about the product specifications needed to meet your standards.

All you're asking is, "What do you need?" Situational questions make it easy for you to initiate the sales conversation. They are nonthreatening and fact-oriented. You're asking the prospect to elaborate on his needs, wants, and desires.

Competitive Questions

This is the second major category of questions you ask in the needs analysis. Answers to these questions give you information about your competition and how well they perform for this buyer.

"How met" is your first subgroup. This refers to how the buyer meets his need (i.e., your competition). It could refer to a past, current, or future supplier. It could also refer to an in-house operation that currently satisfies the buyer's needs. Here are some examples of "how met" questions.

(How met)   How do you currently handle your sulfuric acid needs?

(How met)   Who is your current supplier for sulfuric acid?

These questions elicit information about your competition. You're asking, "How do you meet your current needs?"

"How well" is the second subgroup of competitive questions. You're seeking information about the competition's performance. You want to determine what the buyer likes and dislikes about his current supplier and his goods and services. Is this supplier and product meeting the buyer's needs satisfactorily?

(How well)   How well has your current supplier met your needs?

(How well)   What's been your experience with the sulfuric acid you've been purchasing?

(How well)   What type of feedback have you received from your people who are using this material?

Your objective is to raise the prospect's awareness level that his current way of attempting to meet his needs might be failing him. Avoid anything that might be perceived as sour-grapes selling. You don't want to bad-mouth the competition. However, you do want to provide an accepting climate for the buyer to voice concerns over problems he's experienced. Create an opportunity for the buyer to discuss the problems his other vendors have caused him.

Projective Questions

This is the third group of questions you ask in the needs-analysis stage. Your intent is to highlight the gap between the buyer's needs and how he has attempted to meet these needs. Encourage him to dream a little. Take him to Fantasy Island to consider the ideal buying solution for him. Ask hypothetical or "what if" type questions to achieve this. Ask questions about changes or improvements he would like to make in how he's attempted to meet his needs (i.e., his vendors). Here are some examples.

- If you could change anything about your current supplier, what would you change?
- What would be your idea of the ideal product?
- What would you like to see us do for you that your current supplier is not doing?
- If you were a supplier, what would you do differently?

In each case, you've asked the buyer to dream a little about the ideal solution for his problem. You could take this one step further and ask what effect these changes would have on his business.

For example: "If you could improve something about the service level you're receiving currently, what would you change *and how would that help your business?*"

This question encourages the buyer to elaborate on why he should change his current supplier. The beauty of this question is that he sells himself. The buyer convinces you and himself that there might be a better mousetrap. The next logical comment from the prospect is, "What do you have available that could give me these things I need?" Now he's open to change, and your task is to demonstrate how your product can do this.

A question I often hear in my seminars is, "What happens if the buyer doesn't know of any changes or improvements he'd like to make? What do I do at that point?" Suggest ideas and get his reaction to them. The ideas you suggest are coincidentally the unique strengths your company offers. This scenario demonstrates how to do this.

(Seller)	Mr. Buyer, if you could change one thing about your current supplier, what would that be and how would it affect your business?
(Buyer)	I'm not sure I'd change anything. We're pretty happy with what we have right now.
(Seller)	Let me suggest a couple of ideas for your feedback. How would you improve the delivery time and technical support from your current supplier?

In this example, you draw attention to delivery and technical backup. You focus on two specific areas on which the prospect must comment. It's incumbent upon him to tell you about some changes he'd like to make in these areas. Once he admits that there are some improvements needed in these areas, he opens the door for your presentation. You then describe the features and benefits of your delivery and technical support.

If you scrutinize the logic of the needs analysis, you discover how amazingly simple it is. You're asking three basic questions.

(Situational)	What are your needs?
(Competitive)	How are you meeting those needs?
(Projective)	What would you like to do to better address those needs?

As long as your questions fall into these three categories, you are performing a thorough needs analysis. You evoke the type of information that helps you sell against price.

STRATEGIC OBJECTIVES

Are you wondering how to use the needs analysis to sell against price? Begin with strategic questioning objectives. What do you want to accomplish with your questions? Your first strategic questioning objective is always to gather facts. Your second objective is to begin selling what is unique about your company. This second objective can be satisfied by the nature of your questions. By asking the right questions, you plant seeds in the buyer's mind for a potentially better mousetrap. Your questions spotlight those areas where the buyer might find a better solution to his problems.

By probing with strategic questioning objectives other than selling cheaper, you eclipse the price issue. You minimize its importance and underscore all variables a buyer must consider when purchasing. Here is a questioning scenario you might design for a sales call. Notice I begin with a strategic questioning objective. This adds a sense of purpose to the questions I ask.

Strategic Questioning Objective

To gather facts and plant seeds regarding our unique advantages (our strong technical department support).

Situational Questions

- How often have you found yourself in the position of needing additional technical support?
- Because of the complexity of your process, how involved do a supplier's technical people need to be in your operation?
- I understand that many of your jobs are custom work.
- What do you need from a supplier in terms of customization?

Competitive Questions

- How have you handled your needs for customization and technical support in the past?

- What problems have you encountered in getting the support and flexibility you need?

Projective Questions

- If you could improve the technical support and degree of customization you've received in the past, how would you change your suppliers and what effect would that have on your business?

Armed with this information, you're able to advance to the presentation stage where you tell your story. Naturally, you tell how your technical support and ability to customize can satisfy the prospect's unmet needs. You sell proactively against price by highlighting those buying criteria that are more important. You mitigate the importance of price by raising other issues. Realistically, you have not eliminated the price issue totally, but if you arrange your questions around a strategic objective, you at least put it into its proper perspective: only one of many variables to consider.

Summarize Needs

Once you have thoroughly analyzed the buyer's needs, summarize your understanding of these and put them into your own words. Feed this back to the buyer for his confirmation. When you summarize his needs several things happen. First, you're demonstrating that you were listening to him and understand his situation. Second, you're verifying this understanding of his needs. Third, you're building commitment by getting him to agree to the needs you've uncovered.

When summarizing, begin with a simple lead-in phrase and then recap what you've learned about his needs. When he has agreed to these needs, use them as a springboard to transition to the presentation stage. For example: "Mr. Buyer, based on our conversation I understand you need better lead time, tighter quality control checks, and more flexible shipping hours. Does this cover it? (Yes.) Let's look at some ways in which I feel we can help you achieve these objectives!"

Now, you advance to the presentation stage.

CONCEPTUAL SELLING

Buyers go through many stages in their decision process. First, they agree to a need. Next, they agree to a product, supplier, and so on. Be sure that your buyer agrees first to needing something before discussing your product. This is conceptual selling: convincing your prospect of a need. This happens with your questions in the needs analysis. As you ask questions about technical support and customization, you are gradually selling this person on the concept that he needs to make a change in these areas. Once the individual accepts the fact that he needs more customization and technical support, your job is easier.

A common example of conceptual selling is the confirmed bachelor. His girl friend can talk until she's blue in the face, but he still won't marry. He isn't sold on the concept of marriage. He doesn't recognize the need. The same thing applies to your prospects. If they're not sold conceptually on the need, your task is to sell them on the need and then the product.

Remember, the needs analysis gives you facts, draws attention to buying criteria other than price, and enables you to begin selling the buyer conceptually. Conceptual selling will play a major role later in this book when we talk about different ways to sell proactively against price.

TIPS FOR QUESTIONING

1. Begin by asking permission to probe. It's courteous, and the buyer commits to answering your questions when he approves. For example: "Would you mind if I asked a few questions to better understand your business?"

2. Ask one question at a time (with the exception of the projective question).
3. Ask open-ended questions most of the time.
4. Ask indirect questions to reduce the perceived threat.
5. After you ask one question, pause and let the other person respond.
6. Take brief notes. (You may even want to ask permission to do this.)
7. Begin your needs analysis with a strategic questioning objective.
8. If you sense the other person has a problem in a specific area, pursue it with a follow-up probe. Dig deeper.
9. Interview—don't interrogate. You're not there to fill out a questionnaire. Your goal is to get the other person talking about problems.
10. When constructing your needs analysis, make sure that you ask questions in each of the three strategic questioning areas: situational, competitive, and projective.

CHAPTER SUMMARY

Probing is one of the most important value-added selling techniques you can master. Effective probing opens up the buyer and involves him in the sale. As the buyer becomes more involved in the sale he's more committed to doing something about his needs.

When constructing your questions consider the length of the buyer's response you desire, the risk factor of your question, and whether or not you want to lead the buyer. Also, consider your logic in asking questions. Use the strategic questioning format to help sell the buyer conceptually.

Remember the significant impact your active listening has on the buyer. You're recording a message on that tape inside his head that you genuinely care about his needs. That, coupled with the information he shares with you, gives you a significant edge over the competition.

5
The Presentation Stage

The presentation stage is that part of the value-added sales call where you tell your story relative to the buyer's needs you discovered with your questions. You relate the features and benefits of your product in a persuasive manner, convincing the buyer of the value of what you sell. This means first selling the buyer on the concept of value and then on the specifics of your product.

By presenting your product you raise buyer desire to the boiling point of anticipation. Customize your story to the extent that it appears the product was made especially for the buyer's unique blend of needs.

An effective presentation stage enables you to sell even faster by reducing callbacks. It enables you to proactively deal with objections—to head them off at the pass. When you proactively raise a common objection, you own it. It's yours. The buyer doesn't feel the need to defend it. You've answered his objection in advance. Now there's no reason for him to raise it.

An effective presentation stage gets the buyer excited. Think back to the last new car you purchased. Didn't you get excited as the salesperson described its many features and benefits? You probably took a mental journey in your new car, seeing yourself driving down the street, people gazing admiringly at your newest purchase. You were excited because you were involved and participated mentally with the salesperson. That is an effective presentation stage.

My objective for this chapter is simple: I want to teach you how to sell and speak more persuasively. Specifically, I'll begin by listing some rules for the presentation stage. These are guidelines that can help you come across more effectively. Next, we'll examine three different ways you can discuss your product: claims, features, and benefits. I'll share with you two involvement techniques we use in professional speaking to "engage" an audience. These techniques work equally well in selling. Finally, we'll explore some ideas on how to look at your product to sell added value. I'll suggest some questions for you to ask yourself that will help put you into the correct mindset for a value-added sales presentation.

RULES OF THE PRESENTATION STAGE

Use these guidelines to enhance your presentation. Employ all of these ideas to maximize your chances for success. Each rule has been carefully selected to support a tenet of persuasion. Give yourself the full benefit of the synergism that happens when these rules are used simultaneously.

Rule Number One

Sell what's relevant. This may appear too obvious, but don't let its simplicity fool you. You've just invested a substantial amount of time in the needs analysis discovering the buyer's needs. It makes sense for you to tailor the feature/benefit presentation to answer these needs. Consider the impact it would have on the buyer if you failed to sell what's relevant. The message you send is, "You told me your needs. I either didn't hear you because I wasn't listening or I don't care what your needs are. Just listen to what I think is important about this product!"

Rule Number Two

Sell what's unique. In the strategic value analysis you listed what was unique about your company. It's important to communicate this message to your prospect. For you to justify selling at a higher price, you must be able to make tangible the uniqueness of your product. Stress the importance of these unique factors. Uniqueness makes it difficult for the prospect to make a direct comparison, and this reduces your competition.

Rule Number Three

Stress nonprice issues. Why would you consciously draw attention to something that is not your strong suit? If the price is not your strongest feature, don't use it. If you want the prospect to change his way of viewing your product, don't emphasize those things that hurt your position. Stress issues other than price—i.e., delivery, quality, specifications, technical support, etc.

This accomplishes several things. First, it boosts your enthusiasm level because you're convincing yourself as well as the customer how valuable these things are. Second, your constant reinforcement of nonprice benefits has a shock effect, especially on the price shopper. You're giving him reason to challenge his position. Third, beyond your enthusiasm, you're projecting confidence in the product and the way your company delivers it. And confidence is contagious!

Rule Number Four

Sell truthfully. Take Mark Twain's advice, "When in doubt, tell the truth." It should go without saying that we want to sell truthfully. Unfortunately, sometimes in our moments of excitement we may exaggerate our strengths. We become overzealous and stretch the truth about our abilities. This especially happens in a value-added sales presentation where your primary objective is to convince the prospect that your quality and service are beyond the competition's.

Rule Number Five

Use understandable language. Sometimes a salesperson uses excessive technical jargon to impress the buyer. This could be a big mistake. Circumlocution is the art of taking something simple and making it difficult. An example: desist from enumerating your fowl prior to their emergence from the shell. You could also say, "Don't count your chickens before they're hatched!" It's much easier to understand and not as pompous as the first illustration. Complex jargon confuses prospects. Real value comes from tailoring relevant features and benefits to the prospect's specific needs—not from obfuscation.

Some salespeople express concern over using language that is too simple because they don't want to insult the buyer. Which do you think is worse—leaving the prospect overinformed or confused? Confused buyers rarely buy. Don't assume that the prospect knows as much about the product as you do. It may be the one-thousandth time you've discussed certain features and benefits, but it could be the first time your buyer has heard it. Simplify your message!

Rule Number Six

Get the buyer involved. People who are actively involved in a change process are much less resistant to change. Buyers who are involved in the sale buy quicker and more often because their commitment level is higher. Seek ways to involve your buyer in the sale. Ask questions. Use product demonstrations. Get his feedback on major selling points. Create vivid word pictures in which the buyer "feels" ownership.

Make the sales call an interview. It should be give and take with both parties contributing. Watch for verbal and nonverbal cues that indicate strong interest. When you see these cues, get maximum involvement. Let the buyer sell himself.

Buyer involvement also creates an air of spontaneity in the presentation. You're producing something to match his individual needs. You're delivering a planned rather than a canned presentation.

HOW TO PRESENT YOUR PRODUCT

When describing your product, service, and company, you have these tools at your disposal: claims, features, and benefits. You can use these to tell an effective story, but first you must understand how each works.

Claims are subjective. They are your opinion. They are useful for generating excitement and interest because they reflect your enthusiasm. However, claims aren't the most persuasive tool at your disposal since buyers expect you to feel excited about your product. An example is: "We offer the best service in town!"

As you can see, it allows you to brag and creates some interest on the other end. The buyer may want more information because of this statement. In fact, the question going through his mind is probably "Why do you say you have the best service in town?" It sets the stage for the feature.

A *feature* describes your product. It's factual, objective, and specific. It could be the height, weight, color, or an operational feature such as RPMs. It could also describe the size of your organization. Features support claims and are more convincing because they are specific. Also, you can prove them. They're most substantial and have more credibility. For example, "We offer next-day delivery on orders placed by 3:30 P.M."

You can join the claim to the feature to make a more powerful statement. For example, "We offer the best delivery

in town. By this I mean that any order you place before 3:30
P.M. will be shipped to you on the next business day."

A *benefit* is the perceived advantage of the feature to the
buyer. It's the reason he buys. Benefits generally include
savings of time, money, and space; increased earnings or
profitability; and increased safety or security. It is how the
buyer stands to gain from owning the product.

To determine the benefit of a product, ask yourself these
questions after reciting a feature: "Who cares?" "Why's that
important to me?" "What will that do for me?" Whatever
follows that question is the benefit. For example:

(Feature)   "We offer next-day delivery for any order
              received by 3:30 P.M.!" (So what?)
(Benefit)   "This enables you to reduce the amount of
              inventory space necessary to stock our
              products, thus saving you money."

Join feature and benefit statements with connectors to add
a sense of rhythm that makes the presentation more conversational. It flows more naturally. Here are some connectors
you can use to join features with benefits.

> . . . this assures you that . . .
> . . . why that's important . . .
> . . . this means to you . . .
> . . . which gives . . .

When you combine a claim, feature, and benefit, you've
created a presentation chain. It's one of the most powerful
tools at your disposal. It's conversational magic for salespeople. Here's an example:

(Claim)   "We offer the best delivery in town.
(Feature)   I say that because any order you call in by
              3:30 P.M. will be on your doorstep the
              following workday.

(Benefit)   This means that you can reduce the amount
                   of inventory space needed for our products,
                   which also enhances your cash flow."

The benefit I use stresses the importance of quicker delivery time as it relates to enhancing the buyer's cash flow. When I highlight features and benefits that enhance his market position, improve his cash flow, or give him a safer yet better-quality product, I diminish the importance of price. This works especially well when the questions in the needs analysis initially draw attention to these key issues. The features and benefits then address the needs uncovered earlier. This results in an electrifying presentation.

YOUR BUNDLE OF VALUE

Do customers really buy price? Is this the only thing they seek in a purchase, or is there something else they want? I submit that price plays a minor role in the decision process if the salesperson does his job correctly. Price is only one of several things a customer wants.

Let's explore this concept further. This is an exercise we do in one of my seminars. Participants are told to list ten things customers desire in a product. This is a sampling of how salespeople respond.

Product
Quality
Reliability
Consistency
Price
Availability
Brand
Meets specifications
Variety
Durability
Appearance

What does the customer desire in a vendor?

Vendor
Financial stability
Inventory status
Customer-oriented
Flexibility
Innovativeness
Technical support
Terms
Training
Reputation
Fairness

What do customers desire in salespeople?

Salesperson
Honesty and integrity
Follow-up
Good communication skills
Knowledge
Accessibility
Enthusiasm
Organization
Persistence
Internal selling skills
Service mentality

As you review these lists, what do you notice? Only one of the thirty items is price. And we could have added another five to each column to make it one in forty-five! If only one of thirty items is price and the customer spends more than 3 to 5 percent of his time discussing price, whose fault is it— yours or the customer's? It's your fault, because you've failed to focus on the other twenty-nine things the customer wants besides price.

The remedy seems fairly obvious. Remind the customer of all those things that go along with the price—all twenty-nine! Sell the concept of your bundle of value.

PERSUASION STRATEGIES

There are three things salespeople can do to become more persuasive: sell the "bundled package," review needs and project ownership, and use involvement questions.

The bundled-package concept is the unique combination of product, vendor, and vendor salesperson. It's how all three come together to create a solution for the customer. Selling the bundled-package concept means demonstrating how the product, the company, and the salesperson meet the customer's needs. For example, if the customer is concerned about quality, ask these questions:

- "How does our product quality meet the customer's demand?"
- "How does our company satisfy the customer's quality requirements?"
- "What can I do to ensure the quality the customer wants and deserves?"

As you answer these questions, you're building a convincing story by combining all three variables. For example:

> Ms. Prospect, you've expressed a concern for quality as one of your primary buying objectives. There are three ways we can help you achieve your goal. First, our products perform at 4 percent better than the specs you have given us. This assures you that you'll receive maximum continuous performance.
>
> A second way we assure your quality is that our quality-control department has just initiated a statistical process-control program that reduces interlot variance to less than .01 percent. You'll get the same quality every order.
>
> Our third way of meeting your quality needs is that I'll schedule quarterly customer-satisfaction visits to personally inspect the materials you purchase from us. Again, this ensures that we're monitoring our performance to match your specs.

Consider the impact this approach has on the customer.

You're thoroughly addressing the customer's needs. The repetition of the quality message reinforces your commitment to solve the customer's problems, and your attention to detail reassures the customer that your bundled package is the right combination for her. Compare this multifaceted approach with the singular approach of only discussing quality relative to the product. The latter seems like an incomplete sentence against a backdrop of the bundled-package approach.

If you're really interested in boosting your persuasiveness, fill in the boxes of the presentation matrix. Along the left side, write in the customer's needs. Across the top, write product, company, and salesperson.

Need	Product	Company	Salesperson
Quality			
Delivery			
Technical Support			

Diagram 5-1: Presentation Matrix

By completing each box, you're building a strong presentation chain. You're giving nine reasons to buy from you and your company. Imagine how the customer will react when you tailor your presentation with nine key points and the competition recites three canned responses to the three needs. You'll blow them out of the water with your technique. You're thorough, passionate, and convincing. The competition's not!

Our second persuasion strategy is the review-needs/project-ownership technique. Use this to present the features and benefits of your product while projecting ownership of it. Your objective is to create a vivid scenario in which the buyer actively sees himself owning and using your product .

Preface each feature/benefit statement with a quick reminder of the need it satisfies. This is the review-needs portion. For example: "Earlier you expressed a concern for better delivery because you have limited inventory space . . ."

You then tell the buyer how your delivery solves his problems. Because you will have many needs to address in the presentation stage, you'll need several "lead-in" review-needs phrases. For example:

- Earlier you expressed a concern over . . .
- Another problem you mentioned . . .
- One other problem you had . . .
- Something else that was bothering you was . . .

In each case, follow this phrase with a review of the specific need.

Your next step is to discuss relevant features and benefits while projecting ownership. Project ownership by assuming the other person has already bought the product. Couple this with possessive words like *your* and *our*. Paint a mental picture in which the other person feels psychological ownership of the product. For example:

(Review need)	"Earlier you expressed a concern for better delivery because of the limited inventory space you have available . . ."
(Project ownership)	"One of the things you'll appreciate about doing business

with us is that we'll give you the
best service in town. When you
call your order into our order
entry department by 3:30 in the
afternoon, we'll ship your goods
to you the next business day. This
will help you cut down on the
inventory space you'll need for
our goods. You'll save time,
money, and space!"

In this example, I used several ownership words. I
wanted to create a scenario in which the buyer saw himself
as the proud owner of my product. I began by assuming
that he would place orders with me, and then I told him
about the great service he'd receive.

Here are some examples of "feeding phrases" into the
project-ownership portion of the technique:

- One way we can help you solve that problem is . . .
- Our solution for that is . . .
- You'll enjoy our . . .

The review-needs/project-ownership technique works
great in conjunction with the bundled-package concept.
Begin each feature/benefit chain by reviewing the need all
three things satisfy. If you refer back to the example for the
bundled-package concept, you'll notice that I told that story
with the review-needs/project-ownership technique.

After you've presented several features and benefits using
the review-needs/project-ownership technique, check the
buyer's reaction by asking involvement questions.

Involvement questions are sometimes called trial closes.
They're questions you ask throughout your presentation
stage to test the water. You want to determine how the buyer
feels about your product before you attempt to close. With
the involvement question (trial close), you're asking for an
opinion rather than a commitment. You want to flush out

any possible resistance or negative feelings he harbors. For example:

- How do you feel about this?
- Is this what you had in mind?
- Do you feel this will work for you?

Another way to use the involvement question is to let the buyer sell himself. Ask a more open-ended question regarding a nonprice benefit. Specifically, ask the buyer how a certain benefit will enhance his position. For example:

- "How do you feel our next-day delivery will help reduce the cash flow problems you've recently experienced?"
- "What impact would our additional quality have on your product's position in the marketplace?"

In both examples, the buyer elaborates on why he should own your product. He's mentally conditioning himself for ownership. He's also giving you reasons you can use, if needed, to reemphasize the importance of the benefit.

If you get positive responses to your involvement questions, move ahead for the close. Ask for a commitment. If you get a negative response or hesitation from the buyer, dig deeper and ask questions to uncover resistance.

PRODUCT KNOWLEDGE

If you want to convince your buyer that your product is a great deal, you must have good product knowledge. It's difficult to sell from a position of ignorance. People buy when you tell your story in such a way that it becomes their story. How much product knowledge do you need? At the very least, you need as much as the buyer needs to know to make a sound business decision. In short, you need to be an expert in your product line. Use these guidelines to learn more about your product.

Answer this question: "In what ways does my company (and product) enhance or improve these things for my buyer: profitability, cash flow, image in the marketplace, his credibility to his customer, his service to his customer, the prospect's competitive posture, worker productivity, operational efficiency, product quality, ordering convenience, comfortable usage by customer's employees, morale, safety of usage, and employee relations?"

If you can demonstrate to the buyer how your product can raise morale, productivity, and the quality of his product, do you think price will be a major issue? Of course not. Remember, when the buyer says, "I need a better price," he might be saying, "I need a way to be more competitive in our market. Show me how your product can help me achieve this."

Another question to ask yourself is: "How does my product or service eliminate, reduce, avoid, or help alleviate these customer concerns: product waste; rejection rates, inefficiency; lead time; quality problems; backorders; downtime; risk; internal employee conflicts; employee stress, turnover, or absenteeism; unsafe conditions; morale difficulties or grievances; employee energy level?"

When you spend time learning more about your product, it is time well invested in your career.

CHAPTER SUMMARY

Presenting effectively is not difficult if you observe a few rules. Your goal is to tailor the presentation of the features and benefits of your product to create something unique for that buyer. You want him to feel that this product or service was created especially for him. Be sure to substantiate your claims with features and extend these features into customer benefits. The buyer purchases these advantages your product offers him. You can intensify buyer desire by using the persuasion techniques we discussed earlier in the chapter. Make it easier for him to buy by creating psychological ownership during the call. Involve the buyer with your questions and lower his resistance to change while increasing his motivation to buy. Study your product from every conceivable angle and determine what you offer that is unique. Enhance your product knowledge to boost your sales.

6
The Commitment Stage

The commitment stage of the sale is that point where you achieve your call objective. Sometimes it's referred to as the action step, the close, or the logical conclusion to a series of events. It generally involves a certain amount of detail work to finalize your arrangements. In all cases, it's accomplishing whatever you set out to accomplish.

Some people will tell you that getting buyer commitment is more anticlimactic than they anticipated because the fireworks didn't go off. It was something less than spectacular because there was no magic in it for them. Indeed, that's the way it should be. There are no good closers—just good salespeople. If you've failed to do an adequate job of analyzing the buyer's needs and tailoring your presentation, it's difficult to resurrect interest during the commitment stage.

I prefer the word *commitment* to *closing* because closing indicates finality. Commitment indicates a strong relationship and two-way accountability for a course of action. In value-added selling, you don't close sales; you build commitment to a course of action that brings value to the customer and profit to the seller.

Commitment isn't an end point. In fact, it's the starting point for a course of action that solves a problem. Building commitment doesn't start at the end of the sale but actually takes place throughout the presentation. As you study needs and propose alternative solutions, you're building commitment. The point at which the final decision is made is where you ask for the business.

To avoid confusion, I'll use the terminology *commitment techniques* to describe how you ask the question that results in buyer agreement to own the product. Some call these closing techniques. I still prefer to call them commitment techniques. Remember, though, commitment is something that you build throughout the presentation.

Asking for buyer action is one of the most important steps in the selling process. Nothing happens on your end until the buyer agrees to cut you a purchase order, write a check, or sign a contract. This is what you're paid to do: ask for the business. Don't ever assume that the buyer will come forward and just volunteer to purchase without your asking. It may happen occasionally, but don't depend on it. The buyer may be unaware that the sale is approaching the moment of truth unless you tell him. Ask for buyer commitment, because without it you're unable to provide him with the solution he needs. His commitment brings the solution he desires.

In this chapter, we'll discuss when and how to ask for buyer commitment. We'll examine some ways for you to know when the time is right. We'll also look at how to do it and offer some practical tips for this phase of the sale. In each case, our objective is to gain buyer commitment, achieve our call objective, and secure a profitable order.

Conceive of asking for the order as a two-step process. The first step is asking an opinion-seeking question—sometimes called a *trial close*. What you're asking for is an opinion about your proposal. If the customer's response is positive, ask for a commitment. It's simple, it's practical, and it works! Remember, opinion and then commitment. Knowing when to ask the opinion question is crucial, and this is what the next section tells you.

When to Ask for the Order

Timing is everything in sales. It's just as important for you to know when to ask for the business as it is for you to know how to ask. In this section we'll examine some techniques you can use to determine if the buyer's interest level is sufficient to pursue a commitment at that point. There are two ways to do this: verbal and nonverbal buying signals.

Verbal buying signals are anything the buyer says that indicates a strong interest in owning your product. Additionally, it could be how he says it: a change in inflection or sudden emotion in one's voice. Here are some examples of things one might say to indicate a strong interest in buying.

- "I think it *may* cost too much!" (He's really saying, "Sell me!")
- "How soon can you deliver?" (A sense of urgency is apparent in his voice.)
- "Who pays the freight charges?" (A matter of working out the details.)
- "Is there a guarantee?" ("Reassure me that I'm making a good decision.")
- "Is there an installation charge?" (Working out the details.)
- "I'd like to buy but . . ." (Whatever follows "but" is what you need to address.)

The buyer may indicate interest verbally by repeating strong benefits you've already mentioned. He may start asking more questions—especially those of a technical nature. When the buyer uses possessive words like *mine* and *our* to describe your product, he's bought it. In real estate, they say that when you stop referring to it as a house and start calling it a home, you've bought it. Be attuned to these changes in verbal behavior. Listen for subtle changes that indicate psychological ownership has taken place. Sometimes it's the nuances that tell you when the time is right.

Nonverbal buying signals are things the buyer does to indicate strong interest in your product. Emerson said,

"What you are speaks so loudly that I cannot hear what you say." Be sensitive to nonverbal cues. Nonverbal indicators include the buyer's stroking his chin, leaning forward toward the seller, hand-rubbing, caressing the product or the literature, smiling, giving a sigh of relief during the presentation, uncrossing his arms, and moving closer to the seller. All of these indicate that the buyer is seriously considering owning the product.

In value-added selling, it's especially important to be sensitive to buying signals when you present nonprice issues. Watch for the prospect's interest level when you discuss freight, delivery, quality, technical support, etc. He may tell you that he's not interested, but verify this nonverbally. If his nonverbals indicate strong desire, go with them.

Be perceptive for all of these signals. Listen with your eyes and ears. Be prepared to seek commitment. But first, ask the opinion question. Check his reaction to your ideas. Here are some opinion questions you can ask:

- "What do you think?"
- "Is this what you had in mind?"
- "Will this do the trick for you?"
- "How do you feel about this?"

These are the same involvement questions we asked in the presentation stage. At this point, the answer tells us whether or not to move forward for a commitment. Opinion questions (trial closes or involvement questions) precede commitment questions. I'm aware of my redundancy, but it demonstrates how important the opinion-commitment association is. If you get a positive response to the opinion question, ask for a commitment.

COMMITMENT STRATEGIES

As we go through this list of eleven commitment strategies, remember that each one of these is preceded by an opinion question. Because you've received a positive response, you feel confident asking for a commitment. Demonstrate this confidence in the way you ask for the buyer to act.

Assumptive Technique

With this technique you take a very matter-of-fact approach and assume the sale has taken place. Your assumption is implicit in the statement you make. The logic that supports this is that you want to capitalize on the momentum you've established. Unless the buyer stops you, proceed, because the sale's been made. For example: "If you feel this gives you the quality you need, let's schedule delivery for next Monday." "Since this offers you the shipping flexibility you require, I can have this out here this afternoon if you'd like!"

In both cases, my statement seems like the natural conclusion to the events that preceded it. Notice that I referred to a benefit in the commitment statement. Any time you can include a benefit with your request for action it reinforces why the other person should purchase your idea. It reminds him of the advantage of going with you—the benefits he receives.

Summary Technique

With this technique, you recap the major benefits that you offer the other person and follow this summary with the assumptive technique. Use this to refocus a conversation that has gone astray in the presentation stage. For example: "Our next-day delivery reduces your lead time, and the enhanced quality of our product offers you the opportunity to be more competitive in your market. Let's schedule your first delivery for next week?"

Immediate Advantage

There are two ways to use this technique: the right way and the wrong way. The wrong way is the doomsday technique.

With the doomsday, you try to intimidate and browbeat the other person into buying. You warn him that something ominous will happen if he doesn't act now. You threaten limited inventory, price increases, or any other potentially negative situation. Because of its effectiveness, sales trainers have taught this strategy for years.

Part of the problem with this technique is that it's been widely used and abused. Consumers have become desensitized and in many cases turned off by this approach. They feel backed into a corner to make a quick decision. For example: "If you don't give me an order right now for these goods, I can't guarantee you'll get them on time because we have a limited stock available."

A more positive way to approach this is the immediate advantage. With the immediate advantage, you tell the buyer why it's advantageous for him to press ahead and make a decision to go with you. You're still capitalizing on a sense of urgency but in a more positive way. For example: "The real advantage to your moving on this right now is that because we currently have inventory, we'll be able to give you the delivery you want to stay competitive in your market."

With the immediate advantage, you're stressing the advantage of moving ahead now as opposed to the disadvantage of waiting. It's a more positive approach for your buyer.

Alternate Choice

With this commitment technique, you're asking the buyer to choose one of several options. The logic is that it's much easier for some people to select on a minor point (i.e., color, size, etc.) than to decide whether or not they're ready to buy. My feeling is that if the prospect is ready to buy, he'll buy regardless of how you ask. I include this technique as a convenience for the salesperson. Some salespeople have an easier time asking for the business with the alternate choice rather than directly asking for a commitment. Here are some ways you can use this technique:

- "Which would you prefer: the blue or green unit?"

- "Would you want to go with the 90- or 180-day certificate of deposit?"
- "Do we need a written purchase order, or is your oral commitment enough here?"

As you can see, your logic is an either/or selection. Be sure to present options with which you can live. You don't want to offer a choice of items that would cause you difficulty.

Physical Action

Some sales require the buyer to sign a contract, fill out an application, or complete a formalized purchase order. In these cases, handing the buyer a pen with the contract and asking for a signature is appropriate. Be careful with the wording you select. Try to avoid anything harsh that would turn the buyer off. For example, avoid this type:

- "I'll need you to sign your life away here!"
- "Put your John Hancock here if you would!"

Even though both of these are presented in good fun, the buyer might be put off by your treating his business and commitment so lightly. Try for something softer.

- "I'll need your OK for us to get the wheels turning on our end."
- "We'll need your approval right here to begin your service!"

Also, point out that it's a mutual commitment because you've had to attach your signature to the document also. It creates an ambience of teamwork and camaraderie.

Concession Technique

There are times in sales when the buyer asks you to concede on terms, shipping costs, FOB point, etc. If the deal is good enough for you, don't dismiss this request prematurely.

Pursue it before saying "No!" This is called the concession technique, and this is how it works:

> Mr. Prospect, I'm not sure we'll be able to give you the terms you're looking for, but I'm at least willing to go to my boss and run it by him. In order to do this, I'll need a firm commitment from you because the first words out his mouth will be, "Is this guy shopping or buying?" If you give me a firm commitment based upon our meeting your demands, I'd love to pursue it. Please understand that I can't say "Yes"; my boss will have to OK it.

There are two major advantages to this technique. First, you're going to your boss with a firm commitment for an order. The monkey's on his back as to whether or not he wants to write the business. Second, because the buyer has made a commitment, it's possible that even if you're unable to meet his demands, he'll go ahead and say to you, "You've got the business anyhow, but you owe me one!" It could be easier for the buyer to award you the business than to reopen negotiations with someone else.

Direct Technique

This is a straightforward request for action. There's no doubt what you want. You want the buyer to give you a commitment to act, and he also knows it because of your wording.

- "I'll need your purchase order number to ship these goods!"
- "Where would you like the material shipped?"
- "Where would you like to go with this from here?"

Stall Technique

When you sense that the buyer is hedging or stalling, dig a little deeper. Discover the real problem by smoking out any vestige of resistance so that you can answer the buyer's concerns. The stall technique gives you a systematic way to persist. When you ask an opinion question and receive a dubious answer, try these four questions:

- "You still sound a little hesitant . . ." (Pause and let the buyer respond.)
- "What do you feel must happen on your end for you to go with us?"
- "Do you see any reason at this point why you wouldn't go with us?"
- "Because I'm interested in your business I would like to follow up shortly. How soon can we be in touch?"

The fourth question is your last-ditch effort. If you haven't answered their concerns by then, you need to make another call at a later date. After your first three attempts, any more would be seen as pushy. You need to regroup and come back later.

Probability Technique

You're unsure if the buyer will buy your product. She's hesitating and you want to know why, or at least whether or not there's a chance you can do some business. Ask the buyer to rate her interest level on a scale from one to ten.

> Ms. Buyer, if you were to rate your interest in buying our product on a scale from one to ten, with ten being most interested, what is the probability of our doing business?

If she responds "five or less," you could say, "What will it take to get it to a ten?" If the buyer response is six or more you could say, "Since your interest level is better than 50 percent, why don't we go ahead and schedule delivery so you can begin taking advantage of our quality as soon as possible?" (Or whatever benefit you want to stress.)

Future-Order Technique

There are times when you sell the buyer on your product, but there's no immediate need on his end. Taking additional inventory would not be a good business decision for him. You want a firm commitment for an order that will materialize in the future. Any commitment at this point gives you a greater likelihood of getting future business.

Try this: "Mr. Buyer, since you like the quality of our product (or another nonprice benefit) and our delivery capabilities, can we depend on your commitment to give us a try the next time you order?"

At this point wait for the buyer to say "Yes." Now ask a question that increases his feeling of accountability: "Would you mind if I followed up with you in a couple of weeks just to see how things are going?"

Your second question alerts the buyer that you are going to ask about inventory again on your callback. Because he will face you again and knows it, there's a greater likelihood of his giving you an order in the interim. He feels more firmly committed. Any commitment is better than no commitment at all. He won't want to refuse what he's already promised you. Most people like to keep their word.

If/When Technique

Assuming you're following up with a customer, or just trying to firm up a commitment on your call, this technique works well. Like the other techniques we discussed for "reluctance situations," this technique helps you to identify the likelihood of your doing business with this person:

> Ms. Buyer, because we are interested in your business and would just like to know where we stand, is it a question of *when* you're going to order or is it still a question of *if* you're going to order?

This tells you whether or not the buyer has made a

commitment. In effect, you're asking if she's bought and if it is just a question of time. It's one step closer to a firm commitment. If it is a question of "when" and not "if," determine her timetable and what must happen on her end for the order to materialize. Identify obstacles or potential barriers. Try to do something about them. If it's still a question of "if," dig a little deeper to see if there are unresolved questions or doubts.

CHAPTER SUMMARY

Gaining buyer commitment is one of the most important steps in the selling process. Some argue that it's the most important. For this reason, there's traditionally been a mystique or magic that surrounds this stage. But there shouldn't be. I'll repeat what I said earlier, "There are no good closers—there are just good salespeople."

Knowing when to ask for the business is as important as knowing how to ask for the business. Timing is of the essence. Watch the buyer. Listen with your eyes and your ears. Look for the verbal and nonverbal indicators that the buyer is ready. At that point, ask an opinion question to check his interest level. If the interest level is high, move toward a commitment. If the interest level is low, dig a little deeper.

Using any one of these eleven commitment techniques we discussed can help you finalize the details. I offer a variety of these, not for the buyer's benefit, but for yours. In addition to timing, your confidence level is important when it comes to asking for the business. If you're tentative, the buyer will be tentative. If you're hesitant, the buyer will be hesitant. On the other hand, if you're confident and enthusiastic, the buyer will be confident and enthusiastic. The most important thing to remember about this phase of the sale is— ASK!

THE VALUE-ADDED SALES FORMAT

This chart is to be used to help you put the value-added

sales call into perspective. These are the four steps you go through on each call. You can use this chart to plan your calls also.

Opening Stage
Introductions
State Purpose of Call
Ask Permission to Probe
Needs-Analysis Stage
Situational Questions
- General information
- Specific needs

Competitive Questions
- How met
- How well

Projective Questions
- Ideal
- Impact

Summarize Needs
Presentation Stage
Present Features and Benefits
Involvement Questions
Commitment Stage
Opinion Question
Ask for a Commitment to Action

7
The Follow-Up Stage

At the beginning of this book, I discussed the three phases of the value-oriented sale: planning, implementation, and follow-up. The planning phase prepares you for the value-oriented sale. It gets you ready. The implementation stage is where you execute the sales call: opening, probing, presenting, and gaining buyer commitment to action. Your next step is the follow-up stage.

There are many possible motives for the follow-up stage. First, it could involve your following up on an order to assure satisfaction. Second, follow-up could occur even if you haven't sold anything but want to maintain contact with the buyer. It then becomes part of your overall selling strategy. Third, follow-up involves your performing an autopsy on the sale to evaluate your performance.

The follow-up stage could involve any one of these activities. In this chapter, you'll learn how and when to follow up. You'll learn how to maintain contact with the prospect and follow up without being a pest. You'll learn how to scrutinize your performance on the sales call to learn from your successes as well as your failures. We'll also discuss the

81

obligation of the value-added salesperson to assure buyer satisfaction.

MAKE THIS STAGE WORK FOR YOU

As I mentioned above, you would follow up for one of three reasons: to assure buyer satisfaction, recap your performance, or maintain contact with buyers who haven't made a commitment yet.

As a value-added salesperson, you have an obligation to follow up to assure buyer satisfaction. The customer expects it and deserves it. Because lack of follow-up is a major problem with most salespeople, your doing it differentiates you from the rest of the pack. It's their inertia coupled with your effort that gives you a competitive edge. Follow-up adds value to the product or service.

Follow-up also gives you an opportunity to gather important information about the product and its usage. Is it working to meet the buyer's expectations? Does it do the job it is intended to do? You may gain valuable information about the competition on a follow-up visit. Your follow-up evaluation also gives you an opportunity to explore your applications for a product because innovative customers often find additional uses for a product once they own it. This may result in a new product suggestion.

In your follow-up stage, you can plant a seed for something down the road: a new idea, a new product, or a special promotion you'll run. You could also ask for a referral. What better time to seek a referral than when you're demonstrating good service for a product that is working well for the customer? If things are going well for the customer, ask for a testimonial letter. In this letter, have the customer elaborate on the benefits he's enjoying and the service you're delivering.

When to follow up is always a ticklish question. In value-added selling, there are at least two times when you want to follow up. First, you want to follow up between the time the buyer makes a commitment and when the product is delivered. After making a commitment, buyers often experience some remorse. They wonder if they've made the right decision. When you follow up to assuage their second thoughts, you reinforce a good buying decision. When you fail to follow up, you reinforce their concerns. Follow-up is a little extra service that says, "We deliver the value for which you paid or, you're special to us!" You can either follow up in person, on the phone, or by letter. In any case, the buyer is reassured by your attention.

Another time to follow up is after delivery of goods or services. Ensure that it's set up correctly, that the customer knows how to use it, and that it's delivering the benefits you promised.

Your second major objective in the follow-up stage of the sale is to perform a call autopsy. Check out your performance. Review what you did correctly and what you did incorrectly. It's as important to learn from our mistakes as it is from our successes. By reviewing your failures and trying to learn a positive lesson from them, you mitigate the feelings of rejection. Suddenly, failing becomes a learning experience and you feel more enlightened than rejected. It's important to do your recap as soon as possible after the call while the events are fresh in your mind. And don't limit it to situations where you don't sell. Recap your successful efforts as well. It's just as important to know what works well as it is to know what works poorly.

Here are some questions to ask yourself after the call.

- Was I clear with my objective?
- Did I communicate this objective to make the buyer aware of what I wanted to accomplish?
- Did I control the conversation with questions or dominate it by talking too much?
- Were my questions open-ended and did they follow the needs-analysis format?
- Did the buyer fully understand the needs I uncovered and agree to them?
- How tailored were my features and benefits?

- Did I involve the buyer in the presentation stage?
- How many times did I ask for the order?
- What objections did I receive and did they raise significant barriers?
- What is my next logical step at this point?

This last question seems rather obvious, but most salespeople fail to ask it. As you're completing a sales call, ask yourself and maybe even the customer what the next step should be. It adds direction to your follow-up efforts.

Follow-up also means calling back on potential buyers who have not yet committed to your product—maintaining contact with them. You want to keep your thumb on the pulse to see how soon they will decide. The secret is to follow up without being a pest. Maintaining contact with a prospect ensures that if he makes a buying decision it's in your favor. Follow-up is also one of the more difficult things for salespeople to do because they don't understand the dynamics of the callback.

The format for the callback is exactly the same as for the initial call. You open the call with a few pleasantries. In your needs analysis, review significant buying criteria and seek out additional needs. Review the features and benefits that address the buyer's needs and then ask for some buyer commitment to action. There's no need to complicate this format. If it works on the initial call, it will work on the follow-up call.

When executing a follow-up call on an uncommitted buyer, use these guidelines. I call them "Reilly's Rules for Follow-Up."

1. Whatever time frame the buyer tells you—cut it in half. I have discovered that oftentimes buyers exaggerate how long it takes to make a good decision. The times I waited the full duration, I discovered that they had already taken action—but I wasn't on the receiving end. If they say, "Call back in four weeks," call back in two.

2. Always seek permission to follow up. This has two benefits. First, the buyer knows you will call again and feels somewhat obligated to give you a fair deal. It demonstrates your willingness to serve even without business. A second major benefit is that when the buyer gives you permission to follow up you feel less intrusive. You're not a pest. He's said, "Sure, call me back if you like."

3. Call back for another reason. Tell the buyer you want to follow up to see if he's got any questions, or whatever other reason you can come up with.

4. Call back when it's convenient for the other person. Ask him for the best time to call and you'll feel even less intrusive. You could combine rules number two, three, and four to ask one question: "Mr. Buyer, because I am interested, I'd like to follow up to see if you have any questions before making the final decision. When is it most convenient for me to call, early morning or late afternoon?" When the buyer answers, he's given you permission to follow up. You're not a pest. You're delivering a value-added service.

5. If you sense that the buyer is becoming uneasy with your persistence, explain to him that the reason you're so persistent is you're just interested in his business and want an opportunity to prove it even when you haven't received any yet. You might also point out that your persistence is actually a benefit to him because if a problem surfaces after you do business you'll be equally persistent in finding a solution for it.

6. Establish how many unsuccessful callbacks you'll accept before calling it quits. Don't be a prisoner of hope. At some point, you must change your strategy for dealing with a buyer who continues to string you along. Leverage your time well.

7. Always have a good reason to call. Make the buyer feel at the end of the call that the time invested with you was time well spent.

8. Be innovative with your follow-up ideas.
   - Send news articles of interest (especially about your company).
   - Send premium incentives or giveaway advertising items with your name on it.
   - Mail specialty cards for different occasions.
   - Use the telephone often.
   - Drop off new literature.
   - Do something nice for his office or for his staff.
   - Invite him to your office for a tour.
   - Send business his way.
   - Send copies of testimonial letters you've received from satisfied customers outlining the benefits of your value-added service.

CHAPTER SUMMARY

The follow-up stage is the phase of the sale where one of three things happens. You follow up to ensure that your product is performing well for your customer. Follow-up means reviewing what you learned from your sales experience—good or bad: your call autopsy. Follow-up also means relentlessly pursuing a piece of business for which there is a need. At the same time, it means letting go of those customers who keep you a prisoner of hope.

This stage of the sale separates the top sales achievers from the mediocre performers. Many salespeople downplay the importance of follow-up because it requires effort and time. Follow-up adds value to the sale while differentiating you from the competition.

8
Proactive Strategies to Avoid Price Objections

In this chapter we will focus on some things you can do to avoid price objections by continuously selling value. Selling this way makes you proactive. When you're proactive, you're thinking and acting in advance. Proactive means taking the initiative, being progressive, and anticipating problems long before they happen. When you're proactive, you're forward-thinking in your approach.

There isn't a better time to be proactive than when dealing with a potential price objection. When you proactively sell value, you avoid price objections. They never surface as issues to be dealt with. It's much tougher to deal with a price objection after it's been raised. It's like trying to put toothpaste back in the tube after you've squeezed it out. It's not practical. Dealing with price resistance after it's been raised is also like closing the barn doors after the animals have escaped. The best time to deal with these objections is before they're raised.

Doing things in advance to avoid these objections ensures the likelihood of your success. When you're prepared to handle objections, you build your knowledge base. The more knowledgeable you are the more powerful you become. And the more power you have the more persuasive your communication. The formula is simple: preparation equals persuasion.

This chapter is about becoming more proactive. Specifically, you'll learn how to avoid price objections by employing several value-added strategies. You'll also learn how to enhance your presentation: how to use the correct wording. You'll feel more confident in your approach as your creativity increases. To paraphrase an ancient epigram, "I can give you specific examples and feed you for a day or I can give you concepts and feed you for a lifetime."

C.Y.A.I.A. (COVER YOUR ACT IN ADVANCE)

When we go on vacation, we fuel our car with gas, we buy a plane ticket, and we make our hotel reservations. We plan in advance. Isn't it amazing that everyone does this, but few of us go through this same type of preparation for a sales call? We simply fail to prepare. We don't give ourselves the benefit of planning our value-added strategy in advance. We often wait for price to become an issue and then react to it. We're reactive rather than proactive.

C.Y.A.I.A. means that you must proactively sell value to avoid price situations. Here are several ideas you can use to do this.

Strategic Value Analysis

Before you can speak with authority on value, you must be knowledgeable. You must know your strategic advantages and weaknesses. Knowledge is power. The more you know the more powerful you are. There was a scene in the movie *Patton* where George C. Scott, who played Patton, stood on the hillside watching his forces battle the German army. He smiled and said, "Rommel, you magnificent bastard! I read your book." He had just completed reading Rommel's book and knew exactly which counterattacks to use. Knowledge is power. In building your knowledge base, focus on these four areas: your marketplace or industry, your competition, your company, and your customer.

This is called a *strategic value analysis*. It means analyzing all of those variables that affect how the buyer perceives the value of your product. This information equips you to sell value not price. It builds your power and gives you greater control over the sales process.

Step #1: Market Analysis

Knowing your market enables you to focus your energies on those accounts where you can get maximum return. You can have the best seeds in the world, but unless you plant them in fertile soil, you're not going to sell anything. Know where to call, and stay abreast of new issues, trends, changes, or anything else that could help you sell value. Ask yourself these questions:

- Who are my top six most profitable accounts?
- What three factors do they have in common? (These common denominators help you select other prospects who also have these things in common.)
- What are the current trends in our industry?
- How many market segments do we have, and what are they?
- What are the greatest potential growth areas this year and next year for our industry?
- What outside forces (e.g., economy) are applying pressure to our industry?
- Which buyers of our industry's products are doing well, and why?
- Which buyers of our industry's products are doing poorly, and why?
- What market conditions encourage our goods and services?
- Which mode applies to our industry: growth, maturity, or decline?

You may be able to answer many of these questions off the top of your head. For others you may need to dig a little bit for the information. Read trade journals. Ask your suppliers these questions. Confer with people on the inside of your organization. Talk with your peers. Read business-oriented newspapers. Answering these questions allows you to move swiftly and capitalize on current events. It also gives you information to share with your customer, which enhances your strategic value to him. You're educating him, and he will pay more because of it.

Step #2: Competitive Analysis

This is understanding the strengths and weaknesses of your competition. It's scrutinizing their vulnerabilities and their unique selling propositions. Thoroughly understanding the competition enables you to capitalize on your strengths, which are coincidentally the competition's weaknesses. It suggests an entry strategy for your products and allows you to become more firmly entrenched with existing accounts.

When doing your competitive analysis, don't overlook anything. Don't assume that because you find something particularly insignificant that the customer will. Look at things like quality-control departments, research and development abilities, industry status as leader or follower, customer-service departments, method of delivery or packaging, and the amount of consistent follow-up by competitive salespeople. Don't overlook any of these things. They may suggest weak links with the competition. They could be symptomatic of a greater, not-so-obvious weakness. Don't let your skepticism fool you. Gathering competitive intelligence is not as difficult as it might seem. Here are some ideas:

- Ask your customers what they like and dislike about competitors' products.
- Attend trade shows and gather literature while talking with technical types who attend these shows.

- Have your technical people gather information for you.
- Buy, use, and scrutinize competitive products.
- Review all trade publications for articles as well as ads.
- Talk to your credit people to see what they can find out from their "inner circle."
- Subscribe to computerized information services like the Dow Jones Retrieval Service. They will gather information for you that is already public knowledge.
- Frequent lunch locations and after-hours places that your competitor's employees might use. People talk when they unwind.
- Take a competitor's plant tour if it is offered to the public.
- Ask your suppliers what they know about your competition. If they tell you too much and they're selling to your competition, be cautious about what you tell them because they could be working both sides of the street.

Another quick-reference method for analyzing the competition is the product-comparison matrix. (See Diagram 8-1.)

Following the diagram, list your competitors in the left-hand column. Under the product group, list the specific strengths and weaknesses of each. Compare these with your own strengths and weaknesses to get an objective appraisal of your competitive posture.

Act on what you learn. Build a strong sales presentation around the value of the advantages your company and product offer. By gathering this information, you build confidence in your product and in your company's ability to deliver and service. There's nothing so enlightening and motivating as discovering that the competition is as vulnerable, if not more so, than you. Too often buyers do a wonder-

Product Group: _____

	Competitor	Strengths	Weaknesses
A			
B			
C			

Diagram 8-1: Product-Comparison Matrix

ful job of conning us into believing that the competition walks on water. If that were the case, why are they still talking with and buying from you?

Step #3: Self-Analysis

Gaining objective insight into your own position can be as enlightening as analyzing the competition. Performing this analysis offers several advantages. It's difficult to get blindsided by your competition or buyer when you objectively understand your strengths and vulnerabilities. You're prepared for their assaults because you've given it advance consideration.

An objective awareness of your position enables you to deliver an enthusiastic and realistic presentation of your company and product. You're believable and persuasive. Your confidence from this knowledge is contagious. It's electrifying! What better way to dispel any doubts you might have than to meet them head-on and gather facts?

When performing this self-analysis, ask yourself these questions regarding your company, your product, and yourself:

- What do we do so uncommonly well that we far exceed the competition?
- What is unique about us?
- In what ways are we vulnerable?
- Why do we lose business?
- When we get business, why?
- Under what conditions will people pay more to deal with us?
- Why should someone not buy from us?
- What objections do I normally hear from the customer?

When answering these questions, be absolutely candid with yourself. Don't sugarcoat your responses. Be painfully honest. Try to empathize with your noncustomers. Understand why they don't and won't buy from you.

As I travel across the country, I am constantly amazed at the number of salespeople who cannot tell me what is unique about their products. I have them write down the unique features and advantages of what they sell. More than half sit there motionless. They just don't know. It is your uniqueness that enables you to sell value and command higher prices. Discover this uniqueness and couple it with your competitive knowledge to build a persuasive sales presentation.

Step #4: Customer Analysis

Your fourth step in performing a strategic value analysis is to analyze your customer. Learn as much as possible about what's going on in his or her world. Gather relevant data to customize your presentation. Gathering this information and customizing your presentation increases buyer desire. Take advantage of the opportunities available to collect information about a wide range of topics: people, driving factors behind needs, what their customers expect, their market condition, etc. Consider your buyer's world to be a jigsaw puzzle. Each piece is the result of a question you've asked. Try to construct as complete a picture as possible in your customer analysis. Ask these questions:

- What conditions now prevail in the customer's market?
- How is my customer positioned in the marketplace (leader, follower, etc.)?
- What are his strengths/weaknesses in his market?
- Why does he lose business?
- What do his customers look for in his products? (These are things your customer will look for from you.)
- Who are the key players in this account? (decision maker, user-influencer, and gatekeeper—the person who can say "no" but not "yes")
- What are his buying criteria for service, quality, and price?
- Which areas are absolutes and which are areas of flexibility?
- Why do they continue to buy from one or many sources?

Knowing more about your customer helps you tailor your presentation. Buyers are willing to pay more for customized products because they perceive a greater fit with their needs. There's another dynamic at work here also. You're telling your customer that you value his business enough to go this extra step. Everything you say and do supports this message. When you study his situation and understand how it affects his needs, you communicate empathy with your voice. You operate from a vantage point of insight and knowledge.

Your four-part strategic value analysis is a major building block for the value-added sales presentation. You need this information to speak with authority, enhance your personal value to the customer, and create a significant competitive edge.

Use all of this information that you amass to create a realistic "value picture." Try to visualize how all of these facts come together to form a composite of your buyer's needs and your product's solutions. You'll probably discover that this information will build your self-confidence as well as help you build a stronger sales presentation.

Positioning Strategies: Creating Barriers

Positioning is a concept that was introduced by Ries and Trout in their book *Positioning: The Battle for Your Mind*. They define your position as that unique piece of real estate you own in the buyer's mind. It's what he thinks of every time your name is mentioned. It's the message you put on that tape inside his head. For our purposes, we'll take it a step further and include the concept of creating barriers. Not only do we want to own a unique piece of real estate in the buyer's mind, but we also want to create enough barriers so that a direct comparison with another vendor is difficult. We want to create a significant differential advantage.

By creating this unique posture, significant differential advantage, or position, we enjoy less competition. When the customer discerns a substantial advantage among vendors, price variances are easier to justify. This is your primary benefit for creating a differential advantage. It makes your value-oriented sales job easier. The underlying assumption then is valid: if you offer more, you ought to be paid more.

In considering how you'll go about creating barriers, keep these positioning rules in mind:

1. It happens in the customer's mind, not yours. It really doesn't matter so much what you think about you but what the buyer thinks about you.
2. Positions change slowly over time. It takes a while to create significant barriers, so be patient.

3. Everything we do in some fashion affects our customer's perception of the value we offer. When you're late or on time, when you ship good or bad quality, when you offer good or bad follow-up—all of these feed the customer's perception of value.
4. Value is in the eye of the beholder. What's valuable for the customer may not always be valuable for you and vice versa. Value is a perception created by needs, wants, and desires. Your task is to awaken the desires that create the perception of value you can deliver.
5. If you want to charge more than the competition, you must create greater perceived value.

There are three factors that comprise your unique selling posture: the product, your company, and you. You may not be able to create significant barriers with the product and company because much of that is dictated to you as a salesperson. But that doesn't mean you shouldn't try. Search for significant differences. Seek out opportunities where the application of your product or the way you deliver is different. Create barriers in both areas. Give feedback to your management on changes necessary to reinforce your uniqueness.

You can create barriers before, during, and after the sale with literature, brochures, testimonials, newspaper articles, advertising, or any other tool that enhances the image of your product. Talk to many people within your organization and get their impressions of how you can create barriers with your uniqueness. Because their perspective is different from yours, they might offer suggestions in areas you never thought of.

When considering product barriers, explore possibilities in these areas: quality, delivery availability, reliability, durability, and long-term return. In some way, make your product different from the competition.

When looking at company barriers, consider these ideas: progressiveness, financial stability, technical support, responsiveness to customer complaints and inquiries, service orientation, and flexibility. Again, seek ways to use existing barriers or to create new barriers regarding your company. Once you've identified potential areas for change, sell the concept of differentation to management. It may not be so difficult to change. They could be looking for some ways to make the change just as you are.

The area in which I feel the greatest potential for differentiation exists is within yourself. I believe you can create significant barriers in your selling style so that the buyer is willing to pay more for the product just because of you. You can create such added value with your sales behavior that the buyer's perception of the competition is eclipsed by your professionalism. You owe it to yourself and your company to become so proficient in the following five areas that it would seem ludicrous to the buyer to purchase elsewhere.

Your first personal barrier opportunity is knowledge. You must sound like an expert when you open your mouth. Learn everything from your strategic value analysis and apply this knowledge. Take this a step further and learn as much as you can about business. Become a totally knowledgeable businessperson. Make prudent decisions. Make smart recommendations. Dazzle your buyer with your business acumen—your grasp of good business sense. If the person recommending a higher-priced alternative projects good business sense, it makes a lot of difference in the way the suggestion is received.

Your second personal barrier opportunity is preparation. Are you organized or agonized? Do you plan your moves or go with the flow? Is there a method to your madness? The buyer must sense purposeful actions. He needs to feel that you're moving ahead in an orderly fashion rather than stumbling through the sales process. The buyer judges your after-sale effectiveness vis-à-vis your preparation before the sale. Would you cast off in a boat with a full tank of gas but no rudder? Absolutely not. And neither would your buyer. If he doesn't perceive an organized sales plan that is well implemented, your chances for selling value instead of price are abysmally low. Organize your efforts in such a well-orchestrated plan that by comparison your competition looks like a disheveled mess. It's the combination of your commitment to managing the details and the competition's apathy to detail-management that creates a significant barrier in your favor.

A third area for you to create barriers in is your image. Your personal image and product/company image must be consistent. If your company claims on-time deliveries 99 percent of the time, you can't afford to be late for an appointment. If quality is your major selling point, you must dress accordingly. Dress like a businessperson. Don't expect the customer to accept a quality product from someone whose personal appearance contradicts the verbal message. The buyer may not consciously perceive this inconsistency but, perhaps he senses something on a unconscious level, a gnawing, aggravating kind of sensation that leaves him feeling uneasy about his buying decision. Consequently he procrastinates and then contacts other potential suppliers. This chain of events can occur because of an inconsistency between one's image and verbal presentation.

Your depth of coverage is a fourth area for personal differentiation. Create barriers by your thorough analysis of the buyer's problems. Go beyond the symptoms to the causes of these problems. Distinguish yourself by becoming a "sales sleuth!" Differentiate your style by extensively researching solutions for the buyer's problem. Present options for his decision that reflect your efforts. Live this differential edge by comprehensively following through to reassure the customer that he's made a good buying decision.

A fifth way to differentiate your style and create barriers is to play the game ethically. A recent buyer survey indicates that 96 percent of the respondents look for honesty and integrity as the major characteristics they want in a salesperson. Unfortunately, our profession still employs charlatans and other highly manipulative types, but we can use this to our advantage. Most people feel that salespeople are interested only in one thing: how to get their hands on the buyer's money. Think of the contrast your ethical style creates. It's a benchmark by which competitive salespeople are measured. If they don't meet your standards, you won't have to meet their price!

If you're wondering if it is important to create these barriers with your company and product, the answer is "Yes." Place yourself in the buyer's role. Would you pay more to purchase from a supplier who offers the same product and same service as other vendors without any extras? Of course you wouldn't, and neither will your buyer. If you offer no difference in product or company, then you shouldn't charge more than the competition.

If you're asking, "How important is it to create barriers in my selling style?", here's the answer. It is *vitally* important. In 85 percent of the cases, the salesperson makes the difference in the sale. This comes from a survey of industrial buyers, and we can infer that this applies equally to all forms of selling. Create barriers that make it difficult, if not impossible, for the buyer to make an apples-to-apples comparison, and then you'll be selling value.

Outsmart the Competition

Even David can slay Goliath. You can still beat the competition and even cripple them if you do two things. The best part is that they require no hostile action on your part. You simply work smarter than the competition. First, don't compound the competition's mistakes with your own. If the competition wants to make bad business decisions, let them. Don't stand in their way. Worse yet, don't do what they do. If your competitors want to give away the store, why should you meet them tit for tat? If you choose to play follow the leader, at least follow the price leader—not the discount king. In fact, do you want to follow at all? Be strong and be smart. Sooner or later the competition will discover that they're chasing their tails and that their biggest competition is their own stupidity.

Another way you can outsmart the competition is by

better allocating your sales time. Allocate according to greatest potential return. Even though all customers deserve your value-oriented attitude, not all customers deserve the intensity of a value-added sales approach. Here's a simple analogy to help you determine who your value-added targets should be.

Suppose someone dies and bequeaths you one hundred thousand dollars, with one provision. You must invest it in one of three ways and leave it in that investment for one year. You cannot remove it until the year ends. These are your three options. First, you can put the money in a passbook savings account which yields between 4 and 5 percent interest. Second, you can put the money in a certificate of deposit (CD), which currently pays between 7 and 8 percent interest. Your third option is a jumbo CD that currently pays prime plus 1 percent, or approximately 10 percent. Which would you do? Most people say, "Tom, I'd be a fool not to invest the money in the jumbo CD because I get a much greater return on my investment." And that's the correct answer.

But have you noticed that most salespeople fail to allocate their sales time as they would their money? That's a real paradox since you can always get more money but not more time. Ask yourself this question, "Is this a jumbo-CD customer, a CD customer, or a passbook customer?" Then allocate your sales time accordingly. Spend more time with the jumbo-CD accounts. This is approximately the top 15 percent of your customer base, which represents 65 percent of your volume. The next 20 percent of your revenue comes from the next 20 percent of your accounts, and the bottom 65 percent of your customers represent only 15 percent of your business.

By allocating your efforts according to the return on time invested, you're attending to those customers who deserve the value-added sales approach. Coincidentally, you're working smarter than the competition. This strategic move enables you to focus most of your attention on those customers who deserve the value-added approach.

Outsmarting the competition is good business. Making better business decisions, not following the leader, and allocating your time wisely are good strategic moves. You may find it takes some courage to go against the grain, but the payoff is great. You'll feel better about your job and your performance, the customer rewards your efforts with business, and the competition wonders what happened. Work smarter, not harder.

Use All of Your Resources

Salespeople have tremendous resources available to them. Unfortunately, few salespeople think in these terms, and even fewer utilize the resources. Some of the resources that are available include the research-and-development department, customer-service personnel, shipping-and-traffic department, accounts-receivable personnel, and your plant or other physical facilities. Involve these people or places in your value-added approach.

Take customers on plant tours. Let them see and experience your company's commitment to research and development. Let the customer share in the company spirit. Bring him into the fold and make him part of the family.

Take your support people on calls with you. Have the customer-service supervisor find out how he can make your customer's life easier. Why not have your shipping or traffic manager contact the customer? Is there some way he can make the customer's receiving of goods easier? What impact would it have if your credit manager or accounts-receivable manager made calls with you to hear customer complaints about billing?

In each of these cases, using your resources means gaining more thorough penetration into an account. You're connecting at several levels and becoming more firmly entrenched in the account. As with any of these proactive strategies, this requires a commitment to doing this consistently over a period of time. It's not a short-term strategy. It's something you must do routinely to diminish the importance of price. There's an old maxim that covers this situation: "An ounce of prevention is worth a pound of cure!"

Determine All Organizational Needs

Oftentimes our conversations with the people in purchasing confuse the issue. They stress price, price, price. They forget the real reason they must buy. They ignore the quality, service, and delivery that most companies want and need. Look beyond the obvious need for a competitive price. Ask yourself questions about the needs of other departments besides purchasing. Find out what the people in marketing, shipping, receiving, and quality control need.

Determine the real need for your product beyond what you are told. Ask yourself these questions: "What is it about my product that benefits different parts of the organization?" "Does the speed with which we deliver offer a storage advantage to the warehousing people?" "Does the combination of our quality and service give our customer's salespeople an advantage in selling their product?" Find out what each department needs and sell to those needs.

Generate End-User Support

In marketing, experts discuss push-pull strategies. A push strategy is when you push items through the distribution channel. A pull strategy is where you create strong interest with the end-user, and the end-user pulls, or requests, your products from the distribution channel.

Appeal to your end-users by mailing them literature, sending samples, calling on them personally or on the phone, and demonstrating the benefits of your product. Grass-roots support can go a long way toward minimizing price resistance. Actively seek ways to strengthen ties with the end-user.

When I sold industrial chemicals, we had the ideal product for a pull strategy. We sold acid in a PVC-coated glass jug. The coating prevented the acid from splashing about if the bottle broke, thus reducing injury. When I would show this to the purchasing people (push strategy), they would nod their approval and promise to give it serious consideration. Of course, this was contingent upon the price being competitive with what they currently paid. When I showed this product to the people in the lab who would be using it (pull strategy), they couldn't order it fast enough from the purchasing department.

The question you must address is, "How do I get to the end-user and how do I get their support?" It may be advisable to ask permission from the purchasing agent first to avoid problems later.

Value-Added Checklist

Make a list of all the value-added extras your company offers the customers. I'm confident you'll be pleasantly surprised. We tend to forget everything that we do for the customer. Even great service can become routine if that's the accepted standard of performance. Make a checklist of twenty value-added extras and review them periodically with the customer to remind him of what you're offering. Also, it's a great way to check on yourself to make sure you're delivering value to the customer.

Some creative sales managers use these checklists as guidelines for weekly sales meetings. Each item on the list is used as a meeting topic. You could use this checklist as a weekly sales-objective planner. Select one extra each week to discuss with all prospects that week. It's a simple reminder technique that helps you reap big rewards.

Bundling

This is a concept where you add incremental features and benefits without adding incremental cost to the product. An example of this is the Japanese car. At one time, there was only one way to purchase a Japanese automobile: with tinted glass, wire wheels, six-way seats, and AM-FM stereo.

The "real" advantage was that you got all of those "extras" for one low price. If you were to go to an American car dealer, you discovered that you had to pay more for all of those little extra things. It soon became obvious that the Japanese car appeared to be a better deal. It really didn't matter that all of those things had been added into the base price of the car. What mattered was greater perceived value: something for nothing.

Product features and benefits aren't the only things you can bundle. You can offer service bundling. For example, one major computer firm offers free maintenance when you lease a mainframe computer from them. They have made the differences tangible. Service bundling may offer you the greatest potential yet. You can offer maintenance, training, auditing, consulting, and extra handling at delivery. Sometimes this is called "funny money" because there are no hard dollar outlays on your part. You pay out soft dollars in another area to offer these extras. What can you offer the customer as an extra without charging for it?

Proactive Probing

A few years ago I had some dental work performed. Early during my office visit my dentist asked me how my business was going. I responded, "Great! Things are really coming along nicely!"

About twenty minutes later he said, "When are you going to have the bridgework done that you need?" When he told me how much it would cost. I almost fell out of the chair. I said, "That's a lot of money!" He quipped, "Well, you did say business was good, and what better time to take care of this?" He had me and he knew he had me. He proactively probed, knew business was good, and effectively dealt with what started out as a price objection.

In the needs analysis, I discussed the importance of probing in advance to determine needs and market conditions. When you want to avoid price objections, it's mandatory that you ask questions in advance. Ask about the buyer's sales volume and profitability. Determine how his competition has an edge over him. Get information about how poor quality, service, and delivery adversely affect his company's performance. Gather facts that help you build your case and your enthusiasm.

For example, you could ask questions that spotlight your strengths:

- "What type of technical support do you require?"
- "What special delivery requirements do you have?"
- "How much ordering flexibility do you need?"
- "What terms would make it easier for you to order?"

Gather all of the facts you can before telling your story. You'll have more justification for your price when the time rolls around.

Reinforce Value

This is one of the most important things you can do to sell value and higher prices. Reinforcing value is something that must be done consistently to minimize the impact of price. Reinforcing value means that you seek opportunities to remind your customer just how valuable you are to him. Prove it. Make it tangible. Attach a dollar figure to it and demonstrate your real worth.

One way to do this is to ask your customer for a testimonial letter. Ask him to elaborate on why he does business with you. There's a twofold purpose in doing this. First, you show this to other prospects as a testimonial. Second, as he writes the letter he's reminding himself of how valuable you are. The second reason is more subtle than the first, but it does cause him to reflect on your worth to him.

You can reinforce value with indirect testimonial letters. One financial planner I know uses this technique well. He sends out semiannual progress reports on how well he has served his client family. The report begins with "This is what's been going on with our client family so far this year . . ."

- We've save you $250,000 in taxes.

- We've helped you purchase $750,000,000 in real estate.
- We've created $37,000,000 in new real wealth.
- We've helped seventeen of you cross that "millionaire line" this year.

The list goes on with all of those additional benefits he's delivered in the first half of the year. It is an impressive list of benefits that would make anyone chomp at the bit. The important thing is that he has reminded people of how much value he's delivered. It encourages you to think positively of him.

Another way to reinforce value is to find ways to send business to your customer. When you're an active marketing arm for the customer, it's hard for him to throw up the price issue in your face Maybe you could help your customer move some dead inventory. You might know someone else who'd be willing to take it off his hands.

Another creative idea is for you to make your service extras tangible. Have you ever performed favors about and beyond the call of duty? Have you given free samples? Have you offered free training to your customers? Have you given them products for which there was no charge? Why not send the customer a no-charge invoice to let him see your value? You could attach a dollar amount to the service, samples, or whatever and stamp it with a big, red "No Charge" or "Part of the Service!" Help your customer appreciate the value of your service.

You might want to consider sending out value reports on a monthly or quarterly basis. In these reports, show him how much money your product has made or saved him in that time period. If you sell a product that is more energy-efficient, demonstrate to the customer how much he currently saves by using your model. Value reports encompass any number of possibilities. The key is to attach a dollar amount to the benefit your product saves or earns for the customer.

If you sell through distributors, provide the distributor's

sales manager with a status report of your activity with his sales force. Inform him of how often you call with his people and the end-user business you're pursuing. The same concept could be applied to a purchasing agent. After your visit with an end-user, advise the buyer of what you discussed and propose a course of action. It could be done on the phone, in person, or in written form. It's your effort after the fact that brings value to the sale.

Another way to add value for a distributor is to have your literature customized for him. There's real value in that, and you need to make the distributor aware of it.

Another way to reinforce value is to ask questions on your sales calls that cause the buyer to elaborate on your good service, quality, or technical support. Ask, "How's our delivery been lately?" "Has the consistency of our quality solved your downtime concerns?" Ask these questions when your service is fine, quality incomparable, and follow-up impeccable. It's unlikely that customers will raise these positive issues if unprompted. They'll tell you when you've made a mistake, so let them also tell you when you've done something well. It's good for your spirits and good for their perspective.

Sell Intangibles

One of the most difficult things to sell is something intangible. People can't feel, see, smell, or hear it. They depend more on you than on the "product" to sell it. Continuously selling intangibles means enthusiastically and consistently singing the praises of your company, its flexibility and service orientation, the variety of products and services available, and the research and development advances. You can sell these intangibles by updating the customer on changes that are taking place. Demonstrate your company's commitment to research and development by discussing new products. Share journal clippings and articles about your state-of-the-art technology.

Seek opportunities to reinforce the value of all of the

things you sell. C.Y.A.I.A. is a long-term commitment. It is an ongoing strategy that you develop and adhere to. You could develop a "value reminder plan" for an entire year with each month representing a different segment of your plan. It would all come together like a jigsaw puzzle creating for you a portrait of your company's real worth to the customer. C.Y.A.I.A. requires patience, persistence, and a long-term focus to create a portrait of value.

PRESENTATION IDEAS

You can increase the buyer's perception of value by the way you present your product during the presentation stage. In this section, you'll learn thirteen ways to present your product to minimize the importance of price while maximizing the importance of overall value.

Demonstrate Earnings

Show your buyer how your product actually makes money for him. Demonstrate how paying a little more for your product is a good business decision because your product adds value to his product. For example, you sell medical equipment that enables a physician to perform an in-office lab analysis. In the past, he has sent blood work out, but now he does the same test internally and it's revenue-producing. He's earning additional income because he had the foresight to spend the money to buy your product.

Cut Costs

This strategy closely resembles the first, except here you focus on the savings from owning your product. If you sell an energy-saving compressor, demonstrate how your pump pays for itself in a relatively short period of time.

There is a danger in presenting your product as a cost-cutting item. Once you create a cost-containment mindset with your buyer, the buyer then begins to look for other ways to save money. And guess what? It always comes back to you. The customer has trimmed all the fat in his organization, and now it's time for you to reciprocate. Cut your fat, your price, and your margins.

Rather than stressing cost savings, present your ideas as profit enhancements. This is more than a semantic difference; it's a difference in attitudes. It creates a more positive mindset. You're increasing rather than decreasing something.

Get Agreement to the Product First

Seek active customer involvement in the sale and get him to elaborate on how the features and benefits of your product are an advantage to him. Once you get maximum agreement that the product and its applications meet the customer's needs, discuss price as a matter-of-fact detail. Many sales are destroyed because salespeople erect a price barrier from the start by volunteering their higher price before discussing benefits. They've put the cart before the horse.

If the buyer pushes for a price, tell him that you're not doing him any favors at all by discussing the price without presenting the benefits since he's buying a solution—not a price. You could also tell him that it won't cost anything unless all of the features and benefits are a good match for his needs. Build desire in your product's benefits. If he continues to push for a price, you may have to give it to him to avoid raising his suspicions.

Watch Your Wording

The way in which you present your product has a significant impact on the way the buyer perceives it. When making a presentation, avoid negative language, i.e., language that sets up a negative expectation by the buyer. For example, I overheard a printing salesperson one day talking to his customer. He was getting ready to quote the buyer a price. Here's how he said it.

"Frank, I have a price on that printing you wanted. But you'd better put your seat belt on for this one!" What do you think happened at that point? He set himself up for a price objection, and sure enough he got it.

Avoid other self-defeating jargon as well. When you say things like "list price," "normally we charge," "our usual price is," or "what we like to get is," all of these indicate there's a better price to be had. Don't apologize for the price. Be proud of the value the customer receives. If the customer senses apprehension on your part, you've got an uphill battle.

Someone quoted me a price not too long ago, and the range was $300 to $500. Do you think I was really willing to pay $500 for the item when $300 was thrown out? Be definite when you present your price.

Use Sales Jargon

This principle goes above and beyond what not to say. Use exciting and descriptive words to tell your story. Infuse your presentation with sales jargon that raises buyer desire to the boiling point of anticipation.

If you've ever read a Rolls-Royce brochure you know what sales jargon is. When the auto maker describes the leather selected for the interior, you can't wait to feel its soft touch engulf your body:

> Take the leather, for example. It requires twelve hides to upholster a Rolls-Royce. But they're just not any twelve hides. They come only from cows raised in Scandinavia, where there are no insects and no barbed wire fences to blemish the leather while it's still in the possession of the original owner. Each piece is selected and cut by hand, sewn together. . . .

When the copywriters describe the burr walnut facia, they point out that it could be as much as five hundred years old. Their buyers go to Milan to hand-select each piece that is used. It is then pampered in a humid cellar until needed.

After reading this brochure, you can't wait to stroke this piece of history and art that now serves as your dashboard.

Give your product the same careful treatment. Use colorful terminology. Project ownership by using possessive words that indicate the buyer already owns your product. Create word pictures to emphasize the importance of your quality, service, and state-of-the-art capabilities. Study your product literature. Talk to your technical staff and have them describe your product. Ask the marketing people to help you create a persuasive story. Use sales jargon.

Sandwich the Price

When you sandwich the price, you implant it between the presentation of benefits. You're conditioning the buyer to a slightly higher price but cushioning it with benefits. He mentally associates the benefits he'll receive with a slightly higher price tag. Be matter-of-fact in the way you present it. For example:

> Mr. Buyer, one of the real benefits you'll enjoy with our A-14 compressor is the energy-saving release valve. We calculate that we can save you as much as 48 percent of your current energy consumption with this benefit. Granted, we do charge a little extra for this feature. But the real advantage of this is that within the first year your savings more than pays for the price differential.

From the example, you can see that I put the price issue between two overpowering benefits. These benefits mitigated the importance of price because of the savings.

Price with a Summary of Benefits

In our previous technique, you allude to a price in a non-specific manner. When it is time to be specific with the price, interfuse it with several benefits. Reiterate all of the benefits, and then give the price. For example: "Ms. Buyer, your investment for all of the things we discussed—the energy-saving valve, free setup and delivery, six months of maintenance, and state-of-the-art technology—is $1,975."

I combined the price with a summary of the buyer's benefits. I reminded him of all those things he wanted and received with my compressor. Again, you're putting the price against a backdrop of benefits. This is the right perspective for the buyer.

Cost as a Mere Fraction

If your product is part of a much larger product, you can use this technique. Your objective is to make sure the buyer fully understands that your product is only a small portion of the bigger picture. I was competing for a training contract some time ago. In the probing phase, I discovered that the total advertising budget for a specific promotion was about $350,000. My fee for the training program was only $22,000. When I presented the cost of the program, I pointed out that training his people would cost only about 6 percent of the total promotion. Twenty-two thousand dollars seemed rather insignificant when compared to the overall cost of his promotion.

Make your price a minor portion of the buyer's total operation—a fact that is often obscured by the buyer's reaction.

Miniaturize the Cost to Own

If your product has any type of shelf life, you can minimize the impact of price by reducing it to the ridiculous. You could talk in terms of cost per unit, cost per day, cost per application, or cost per test. An example is, "Dr. Jones, the cost of this instrument with all of the features and benefits you wanted is about $1.20 per test. At the same time, you'll be able to charge your patients $10.00 per test—earning a profit for yourself and saving your patients $5.00 per test over what they currently pay to have this work done!"

My primary objective was to miniaturize the cost to own (not the cost to buy) this piece of equipment. Notice that I broke it down to cost per test. The same thing could be done on cost per day, for example. I also presented the cost to own with the benefits the doctor wanted and demonstrated how she could make money with it. This is combining three proactive strategies we've discussed.

There are two ways you can miniaturize price. Either discuss the whole cost of owning your product or discuss the difference in price between your product and a competitive brand. Miniaturize the price differential. If the cost of your product is $300 more than the competition, reduce the $300 to the ridiculous.

Analogize

This technique requires that you know a little about the other person's business. Tactfully point out that spending money for your product is a wiser investment than other purchases she's made in the past. In the previous technique, I used an example with a physician. Let's go back to that situation and analogize:

> Dr. Jones, the real advantage of owning this in-office test equipment is that it will earn money for you rather than cost you money. You mentioned earlier that you recently spent $4,000 on a copier. That's a fixed expense. It will cost you to own that copier. Our analyzer will not only pay for itself, but it will actually help pay for the copier you purchased earlier this year.

My objective was to point out how well my product compares to other buying decisions she's made in the past. Don't rub it in. Rather, use those purchases to your advantage.

If you sell advertising, here's how you might analogize.

> Mr. Buyer, you've invested a great deal of money renovating your store, which makes it pleasant for your shoppers when they're here. Our enhanced advertising

campaign is designed to help you get more people in to see the renovation you've done. Our objective is your objective. We want to help you get enough new prospects to pay for your renovation.

As you can see from both examples, I've contrasted the earning revenue for the buyer with some current situation that's costing him money. It's a subtle dynamic that creates motivation to change. To employ this method, look for things on which to draw analogies, such as drains on business, capital investments, advertising, and employee training programs. Use these as springboards for your analogies.

Use Testimonials

Using the name of someone who benefited from paying a little more for your product oftentimes sways an opinion. This is especially true when it's a well-known person. The more credible the testimonial is, the greater your chances for success. I know someone who leases the most expensive office space in town. He has a wonderful testimonial that he uses to justify charging more for plush offices.

One of his tenants, a medium-sized law firm, was able to recruit the top three graduates from a major law school. The reason these talented young attorneys went with this medium-sized firm is that the expensive offices broadcasted that this firm was "on the move"—the partners were shakers and movers.

This story could be told on each and every sales call as living proof of some of the less obvious benefits of hanging your shingle in a plush office environment.

Think and Talk Long-Term

One of the things I've noticed about price shoppers is that they tend to be short-term thinkers who don't give much thought to the future. Their immediate concern is to solve a supply problem as cheaply as possible and as soon as possible. Your task is to get their minds off instant gratification by pointing out long-range benefits. Discuss the long-term advantage of owning your product.

Price shoppers have tunnel vision. You need to expand their peripheral vision by raising their awareness level of all those factors that influence the buying decision. Make them aware of service needs, quality needs, and so on. Think and talk about how your product will help them one year, two years, and even five years down the road. Explain how your product is a good long-term decision that is consistent with their long-term objectives.

In some industries, it's highly possible to demonstrate the real value of a product or service in hard dollars. If your product fits into this category, use value examples. Focus on the return (long-term) value. Use actual numbers that substantiate your claims. For example:

Value Analysis

	System A	System B
Acquisition Cost	$18,795.00	$13,770.00
Annual Energy Costs	$675.00	$1,405.00
Product Life Cycle	15 years	10 years
Trade-in Value	25%	0
Annual Cost to Own over Product Life Cycle	$1,928.00	$2,782.00
Trade-in Value	$4,698.75	0

(Diagram 8-2)

On the surface, System B looked more attractive because of the low acquisition cost ($5,025 less than A). Upon further analysis, System A is the better long-term decision because it's cheaper to own: acquisition cost plus product life energy costs divided by the number of years in service. Besides, System A offers a trade-in value. System B doesn't.

Using value-analysis examples can be very persuasive on a sales call. Demonstrating your cost to own rather than cost to acquire is a long-term strategy. Good businesspeople understand this and accept it. Price shoppers tend to be short-term thinkers. Your task is to clarify their vision to help them see the long-term benefits. Remember, they plan to own it for longer than just the day they purchase it.

Present in Its Best Light

How many times have you made a presentation under less than ideal circumstances? Price becomes an issue when the customer doesn't see a product at its best. Check the lighting and room temperature. Have clean literature. If you're demonstrating equipment, try it out before showing it to the customer. Watch out for the small details. Use a proposal cover rather than just stapling a few pages together. If you're conducting a plant tour, make sure that the area is clear and clean. Clean all equipment before you show it. If you use slides or overheads, make sure they are in the correct order. In a very positive and optimistic way, play to Murphy's Law. Be sure there are no surprises when it comes time for the presentation. When everything clicks the way it should, price becomes less of an issue for the buyer.

The wording you select, the way in which you present, and the analogies and testimonials you use will have an influence one way or the other on the sale. Watch your wording and presentation technique to ensure that it's a positive impact.

CRITICAL IMPACT AREAS

When preparing your value-added sales strategy, look for ways to do it better than the competition. Try to make the customer's life easier as a result of doing business with your company instead of the competition. We prioritize customers as A, B, or C accounts or jumbo CDs, CDs, and passbook accounts. Customers also prioritize vendors as A, B, or C. Are you an A, B, or C? Try to be an A vendor to those accounts where you want to be an A vendor.

One way to do that is by asking yourself questions to determine how you can make a real difference in the customer's business. In every business there are certain areas where a vendor can favorably influence how a customer operates. These are called *critical impact areas,* and they include things like ordering, receiving, marketing, distribution, and research. Ask these questions to determine how your company could add value and have a favorable impact on your customer's business.

1. How can we help the customer better understand his problem?
2. Is there a way we can help the customer collect all relevant information regarding his problem situation?
3. In what ways can I help the customer design specs for his problem situation?
4. How can we help get information regarding our solution to all relevant parties within the customer's business? (i.e., playing the coordinator role)
5. What can our company do to make ordering easier for the customer?
6. How can we package or ship our goods to make the customer's life easier?
7. Is there something we can do to help our customers receive, warehouse, or ship internally the goods that we sell them?
8. How can we expedite returned goods, issue credit, and reship with least negative impact on the customer?
9. What can we do to help the customer use, convert, or supply our product more efficiently and productively? (i.e., gain quick maximum usage of our product)
10. If service concerns arise after the sale, what can we do to expedite quick resolution of these concerns?

If your customer sells to someone else, ask these questions also.

11. How can we help our customers get their message out more effectively?
12. Can we do something that expedites and simplifies the end-user's ordering from our customers?
13. How can our company help our customer in distribution of his (and our) product to his customers?
14. Is there a way we can help the end-user get quick and courteous service after the sale?
15. Do we need to concern ourselves with end-users needing repair or replacement parts, and if so, how do we do it?

CHAPTER SUMMARY

Being proactive means never having to say you're sorry! When you're proactive, you deal with fewer objections—especially price objections. It means being so well organized that price does not become the major issue. It's covering your tracks in advance.

Selling proactively is a long-term commitment on your part. It will take a while for you to change the buyer's perspective, so don't expect overnight results. Creating this posture of value requires some time on your end. Be patient. Selling value is like painting a beautiful portrait. You do it one brush stroke at a time. Every proactive step you take is one more brush stroke. Remember that it's more difficult to deal with a price objection after it's raised than before it's raised.

9

Reactive Strategies for Dealing with Price Objections

B eing reactive means responding to an existing situation. Reactively handling objections means you wait for the objection to surface and then address it. This concept refers to time—not assertiveness. Just because you're reactive doesn't mean that you're caught by surprise. It only means that you respond after the fact. In most cases, you probably anticipated a price objection and are prepared for it.

That's what this chapter is all about: preparation—being ready for a price objection. It means projecting yourself mentally into the rejection situation so that you're ready for whatever comes your way. Preparation builds your self-confidence. It allows you to be persistent without being a pest: tenacious in a nonthreatening manner.

You'll learn a simple three-step communications model that will enable you to hang in there beyond the first "No!" You'll be able to assertively and confidently respond to the buyer's doubts and concerns. Specifically, you're going to learn twenty-one ways to respond effectively to the buyer's price resistance.

TIPS FOR HANDLING OBJECTIONS

Before we get into the mechanics of handling an objection, it's important to understand a few basic concepts. Here are some things that can make your life easier in this situation.

Divorce Your Ego from the Sale

Remember that when the customer rejects your product it's not a direct assault on you. The customer hasn't said that you're a crummy person and wants nothing to do with you. For one reason or another, he's not sold on your product. Don't get defensive, and don't argue. I don't know any salesperson who won a sale by winning an argument with the customer, though I do know several salespeople who won the argument and lost the sale. Be tactful with your responses. Objections represent tenuous situations at best.

Create an Objections File

One way to be prepared for an objection is to have an objections file with potential responses for each objection that could be raised. Being prepared builds your self-confidence. When you have two responses, you can rely on the second response to do the trick if the first one doesn't. Update your file regularly by adding new objections and responses. Review previously used responses and change the wording if appropriate. Why depend on your mind to store all this material? Make a commitment to yourself to create this file.

Anticipate Objections in a Positive Way

They will happen. It's an occupational hazard, and there's no way to get around it. If you anticipate (not create) objections, it allows you to maintain a more positive mental attitude because you're not thrown off guard by them. You know and accept that they'll happen.

Help the Buyer Save Face

If the objection indicates that the buyer misunderstands what you've presented, give him an opportunity to save face. You may even want to assume partial responsibility for this yourself. For example, you could say, "Maybe I didn't explain this fully enough" or "How about if we go over a couple of things again? I could have missed something." Exonerate the buyer and give him a chance to bow out of a situation gracefully. Your tact will be rewarded.

Listen with All of Your Senses

Be totally perceptive. Listen for what's being said as well as what's not being said. How does the buyer express his objection? What is his mood? How tentative is his concern? Try to fully understand the emotion as well as the facts. Observe the nonverbals.

Be Persistent

Seventy-five percent of all salespeople quit on the first "No!" Another 5 percent quit on the second. If you persist until the third one, you'll be in the top 20 percent of the selling profession. The key is to be persistent without being a pest. You can achieve this if you use the three-step communications model that appears in the next section.

Don't be caught off guard by objections. They are going to happen. It's an occupational hazard. If you're prepared, there's no reason to fear them either. Preparation will boost your enthusiasm and knowledge will boost your power: the combination of these two will boost your sales!

THREE-STEP OBJECTIONS MODEL

The dynamics of dealing with an objection are the same regardless of the nature of the objection. You can use the model presented in this section for any objection you encounter. However, the major emphasis in this section is how to quell price objections. There are three steps in the process: clarify, buffer, and answer.

Clarify

When you clarify an objection, you want the other person to expound, elaborate, or discuss his concern more fully to build your understanding and ventilate his emotion. If he elaborates, it gives you time to think of a response and the buyer may even talk himself out of an objection.

Clarifying generally involves one of two strategies. You can either ask an open-ended question about the objection or you can restate it in your own words, making the objection a question. For example:

(Objection)	"Your price is much higher than the competition!"
(Open question)	"When you say we're higher, could you be more specific?"
(Restate)	"Is it a question of our being justified in charging more than the competition?"

When clarifying a price objection, probe a little deeper to discover his motivation. First, ensure that the buyer is making an apples-to-apples comparison. Is the product he compares to yours exactly the same as yours? Second, is the buyer concerned with the total cost of owning your product or just the acquisition cost? The cost to own includes operating costs, the amount of money you can save a buyer, the amount of money you can earn for the buyer, and the life cycle of the product.

Third, determine if price is the buyer's only consideration in purchasing your product. Fourth, check the buyer's expectations. Unrealistic purchasing objectives could be motivating this price objection. Your fifth concern should be the availability of funds. Your price may not be too high for the value you deliver. It's just too high for the budget this person has available.

A sixth concern is if the buyer wants a better price to be more competitive in his marketplace. He may think that the only way to compete is by offering a better price. You might be able to give him other ideas on how to compete with nonprice issues. A final concern is whether or not the person to whom you're talking is the buying authority. Can he say "Yes" and "No"?

Clarifying is digging deeper. It's probing to find out if there are any additional concerns. When you clarify, you want the other person to discuss his feelings openly.

Clarifying means that you're in the ask rather than the tell mode. When most salespeople hear an objection, they go to the tell mode and try to overwhelm the customer with prepared rebuttals. This is not as effective as going to the ask mode, which gives the customer an opportunity to expound while defusing any adversarial tone. Remember, ask rather than tell.

Buffer

The second step in dealing with an objection is to buffer it. This means showing partial agreement, empathy, or understanding for the other person's concerns. By demonstrating this concern, you're saying to the buyer, "I'm on your side. I understand your concerns." Your empathy shifts psychological ownership of the objection. You're saying, "We're in this together." Here are some examples for buffering an objection:

> "I understand your position."
> "I hear you."
> "Yes, money is one concern."

Notice that in the last one I did not say, "Don't buy because our price is too high." I said that money is one concern—not the whole ball of wax—just one! There are other things to consider.

When you combine the clarifier and buffer, your dialogue flows smoothly. For example:

(Objection)	"You're charging more than I thought we'd have to pay!"
(Clarify)	"What did you think you'd need to pay for this?"
(Buyer)	"About 75 percent of what you're charging!"
(Buffer)	"I can see why you're concerned. I believe in that case I'd feel pretty much the same!"

Here's an example of how to use this model with a non-price objection.

(Objection)	"I don't like your delivery schedule!"
(Clarify)	"What is there about the schedule you dislike?"
(Buyer)	"We need a twenty-four-hour delivery, but you deliver only during regular business hours!"
(Buffer)	"I understand. That is a legitimate concern."

One word of caution is to avoid the yes/but technique. When you use the word *but*, it tends to negate anything preceding it. It's also argumentative. Also, avoid *however* and *although*. They're multisyllabic ways of saying *but*. Review the following yes/but buffers and consider how the "but" discounts the empathy:

"I understand your concerns, Ms. Prospect, but there is another way to view this!"
"I hear you, but look at it my way."

Both are argumentative and telegraph that you're preparing to "slam-dunk" the customer. You can always use the word *and* versus *but*. For example:

"I understand your concerns, Ms. Prospect, and there is another way we can approach this."

"I hear you, and let's examine another option."

The yes/and technique is much softer and it allows you to assert your position in a nonargumentative manner. Everyone who attends my seminars tells me that this is the toughest habit to break. Don't despair—it's tough, *and* you can do it.

If it seems like you're left suspended after the buffer, you are! You've stopped in the middle of a thought. The next step is to answer the objection with your response strategy.

Answer

After you've clarified and buffered, answer the objection with one of several strategies. In general, there are four ways to answer any objection.

First, you may need to inform the buyer. Give him additional relevant features and benefits regarding your product or company to either convince him or correct a misunderstanding of your product, company, or service. In either case your task is to provide additional information to convince him that your product is a good match for his needs.

A second strategy is to review the buyer's needs. Maybe he objects because he just doesn't feel he needs what you sell. It makes sense at this point to go back over his needs and review buying criteria. The review-needs strategy works well when the other person hesitates or stalls. When you review needs, ask the buyer to reiterate what's important to him. This increases his motivation to change.

A third strategy is the alternate-advantage overload. If there's a particular feature that the buyer dislikes, overshadow it with the other features he desires. Your objective is to demonstrate how the buyer is making a relatively small trade-off to get all of the other benefits he really wants. Embellish your presentation with these features and benefits to increase his desire enough to offset his reluctance.

Your fourth strategy is to reverse the objection. When you

reverse it, make the objection the reason why someone should buy your product. For example, say, "Ms. Buyer, the fact that you are hesitating indicates to me that you want to make a good buying decision. If that's the case, that's exactly why I feel you need to go ahead with our product since we've demonstrated its superiority relative to your needs." At this point, reemphasize the specific features and benefits that are an advantage to the buyer.

Any of these four answer strategies requires that you retrace your steps to an earlier stage of the selling process. You'll either go back to the needs analysis to generate additional motivation to change or you'll return to the presentation about your product. If you conceive of your answer strategy as reentry into a previous stage of the sale, it flows smoothly. If you're unable to sell successfully on this call, your answer strategy may represent a follow-up call objective—the reason for your next sales call.

HOW TO ANSWER PRICE OBJECTIONS

In this section, I'll outline several ways you can respond to price objections. You would use these strategies as your third step in the objections model. I suggest that you try to understand the concept fully without fixating on the wording I use. If the words don't work for you, change them, but use the underlying concept. You could consider some of these techniques to be proactive as well as reactive. The only thing that changes is your wording.

The Subtraction Method

This strategy is based on the assumption that you can make the buyer aware that paying less brings with it certain consequences. It works especially well if you have lower-quality goods to sell or can reduce the service level you offer. The buyer becomes painfully aware that there are less expensive options available to him. For example: "Mr. Buyer, if your primary concern is money, maybe there's a

way to get some of the quality or service out of what we sell
to meet the financial constraints you've established."
Another example is, "If your major concern is acquisition
cost, let's pursue some ways to reduce this by removing some
of the things you feel you won't need."

At this point, outline some of the alternatives for the
buyer: less quality, no shipment, no technical support,
slower delivery, COD, etc. Illustrate the trade-offs the buyer
must concede to pay a lower price. Naturally, your objective
is to illustrate that if you pay less, you get less. You don't
really want to remove value as your first option. It's better to
convince buyers that subtracting this value has a negative
effect because they get less, but if they can survive with less
and you are able to substitute, go to it.

Cast Doubt

When you cast doubt, you want to make the buyer painfully
aware of the consequences of not receiving the full advantages you offer. Be careful not to react with a sour-grapes
attitude. By the same token, don't be so subtle that she
misses your point. Aim for something in the middle. For
example: "Ms. Buyer, we know what it will cost for you to
invest a little more and go with our guaranteed delivery,
quality, and service. I guess the only 'unknown' at this
point is what it would cost *not* to have this security we
offer." Your objective is not to intimidate but to point to the
obvious impact of not buying something that she needs.

Reinforce Quality

With this strategy, you reiterate the unique features and
benefits you offer. Refer to the quality of your product.
Confidently tell the buyer that your company has decided
that selling quality at a higher price is a better strategy than
selling at a lower price. For example: "Mr. Buyer, we made a
decision a long time ago in our market that selling you a
quality product at a higher price was a better strategy for

both of us than selling you something cheaper that wouldn't do the job."

At this point, demonstrate how the buyer actually loses by going with something of lesser quality. In effect, you're saying, "There's no apology for quality or service." It's much easier to justify a higher price one time than to continually apologize for the things you can't do for the buyer.

Hypothetical Questions

With this strategy, you'll also focus on those unique things that you offer, but you lead to them differently. Make it a question that a buyer might ask. For example: "Ms. Buyer, many of the people with whom we currently do business initially asked the same question you're asking: 'Why should we spend more with you than the competition?' Would you like to hear what they've discovered?"

At this point, embellish the uniqueness of your product. Tell all of the reasons why you're worth more than the competition. Elaborate on your strengths and translate these into customer benefits. At this point, it makes sense to use testimonial letters from people who paid more to go with your product and are happy they did.

Trial Close

When you trial close on a price objection, you want to find out if there is any other reason why the buyer might hesitate. Dig a little deeper, and try for any commitment at this point. Find out if the buyer would buy if he had the money. Determine if money is the only variable causing him to hesitate. For example: "If you had the money (budget), would you go with us? Why?" or "Is the money the only reason you wouldn't go with us?"

Notice that with the first question I asked the buyer why he would go with me. I want him to tell me why my product or company appeals to him. Get him to elaborate, and he might sell himself on paying a little more. The trial close may even tell us if the other person is being candid. We may uncover an area of flexibility that would enable us to work with the customer.

Project Off Price

Draw the buyer's attention away from the price. Get her to elaborate on your company and product in a price vacuum. Divorce yourself from the price issue altogether and encourage the buyer to sell you on you! For example: "Ms. Buyer, if you were to make a decision today on any and all variables other than price, who would you go with, and why?"

Another example is: "Ms. Buyer, what would cause you to pay more for the product than you had originally anticipated?"

I've encouraged the buyer to dream a little by putting her into a hypothetical situation. While she's responding, two things happen. First, she'll convince herself that there are far worse things than paying too much. Second, it gives you information and time to think of an appropriate response to her answer.

Sell Loyalty

If you've taken care of your customer time and again, you have a right to assert yourself. If you've delivered a quality product with unparalleled service, you have an obligation to sell past performance. You owe it to your company and yourself to sell loyalty.

A friend of mine who is the director of purchasing for a large company in St. Louis shared this story with a group of salespeople one day. His current steel contract had expired and his company was going out for bid. His current supplier quoted a price about 10 percent higher than everyone else's. My friend said to this salesman, "Frank, your prices are too high. You need to go back to sharpen your pencil some more!"

Frank didn't get rattled. Rather, he opened his briefcase and removed a stack of pink slips. This was his record of all the things he had done for this customer over the past year. He placed this stack on my friend's desk, and my friend asked what they were. Frank replied, "Remember last year when you called for all of these favors—above and beyond the call of duty? I kept a record of them to make sure you got the kind of service you really deserve." My friend, the buyer, told him without hesitation that he had the business again that year at the quoted price.

My friend wasn't offended by this assertive approach. He said, "Here I was trying to chisel this guy out of 10 percent, and he reminded me just how valuable he was to me!" Frank sold value and loyalty by reminding the customer of the special favors he performed.

Use Success Stories

This is also a strategy we discussed in the proactive chapter. If someone else has benefited from your product even though it costs more, tell the customer about it. Acknowledge that your price is higher and that other people found it made sense to pay a little more for your product. Be specific with your success stories, and use testimonial letters if they are available.

Analogize

In the proactive chapter, we also discussed using analogies. This works equally well as a reactive strategy. If the buyer objects to your price, point out how spending money in other areas of his business also made money for him. If he has spent money on equipment that costs him instead of earning money for him, tactfully point that out also. For example, if the customer has set a precedent by spending money to train some of his employees, it's easy to point out that investing in the other employees also makes good sense. If the customer has spent money in remodeling, it makes sense to allocate funds for advertising to draw people in to see the work that's been completed. Ask questions in all areas of this person's business. Be perceptive. Look for these opportunities.

Risk of Cheapness

When you use this technique, draw attention to the potential risk factor that the buyer experiences when going with a less expensive alternative. Make the buyer aware that it could negatively affect his business. One word of caution is not to bad-mouth the competition. You don't want to sound like someone who is moaning because you're about to lose some business. Ask the buyer which poses a greater potential risk: paying more than he anticipated or getting less than he needs to do a good job? For example: "Mr. Buyer, considering the image and reputation you've built in the marketplace, which do you feel offers you a greater potential risk at this point: paying a little more than you anticipated or receiving less than you need to help you achieve the results you want?" In this example, I associated paying less with getting less. His reputation could be tarnished by skimping at this point.

Buying Dissonance

When you use this technique, you're appealing to the buyer's business acumen. You're addressing the issue of realistic buyer expectations. You want him to admit that his expectations may not be realistic and perhaps he should reconsider his position. Highlight the discrepancy between what he wants to pay for and what he really needs. For example: "Mr. Buyer, is the quality (service, delivery, etc.) you're willing to pay for consistent with what you honestly feel you need to do the job correctly?"

You're really asking if it makes good business sense for you to offer all that he needs for such a minimal cost to him. Beyond that, you're asking if he really thinks it's feasible for anyone to offer such a deal. If he's an educated buyer, he'll probably grin and bear it. With the uneducated buyer, you may need to do some direct comparisons with competitors' products to demonstrate the real value of yours.

Reverse

Earlier in this chapter, we discussed reversing an objection. When you reverse a price objection, make the higher price the reason why the buyer should purchase your product. For example: "Mr. Buyer, the fact that price is such a concern for you indicates that your revenues are not exactly where they should be. And, that's exactly why you should go with us, because our product is designed to help you increase your revenues!"

I have two caveats for using the reversal. First, practice this technique several times. Add a few pauses and keep the pace slow. When salespeople use a reversal, there's a tendency to be flippant with the response. Guard against this. Second, after you reverse the objection you need a strong feature-benefit presentation to substantiate what you've just said. Don't rely on the reversal statement alone to sway the buyer. Back it up with facts. Look for opportunities to use the reversal, because it has great value as a shock treatment with the buyer.

Alternate-Advantage Overload

In the general response section, we discussed this answer strategy. Acknowledge that your price is a little higher and then reiterate all of those features and benefits that overshadow the price issue. Embellish this part of the presentation. For example: "You're right when you say we're a little higher. We are! And because of that, we're able to give you all of those additional benefits that you wanted! . . ." At this point, enumerate all of the buyer's wants, needs, and desires, and show how the product meets these needs.

Competition to Meet Your Standards

Sometimes the buyer will tell you that if you meet a competitive price you can have the business. Think through this situation; there's a flaw in his logic. If the buyer wants to do business with you, there's a good reason why. Maybe you offer better service, delivery, or quality. If that's the case, why shouldn't the customer pay for it? If your product and service are that good, you should be paid accordingly. Call this to the buyer's attention. Here are two ways to do this.

First, ask him why he wants to give you the business. Then explain that you're no different than him. If you offer more, like him, you expect to be paid more. Reinforce that this is a prudent business decision on your part.

The second way to deal with this situation is to suggest that rather than having you meet the competitor's price, he should have the competition meet your level of quality and service for what they currently charge. For example: "Mr. Buyer, I've got an idea that could make you a double winner. Instead of our meeting the competition's price for this product, why not get them to match our quality, guaranteed service, and technical support—all for what they currently charge?"

Your objective is to stand fast by the quality and service your company offers. Reiterate your commitment to these features. Demonstrate good business sense.

Discretionary Funds

Some price objections hinge on the individual's lack of budget or funds available for purchase. One option is to probe to find out if there are funds available in other areas that could be used for this purpose. Often, suggesting this to the prospect will encourage her to consider alternate means of financing. For example: "Ms. Buyer, it's been my experience in business that most people have discretionary funds available if they feel convinced of the value of an idea. Does this apply to your situation as well?"

What you might discover from this is that the funding is available, but there's another reason for the buyer's hesitation. I confronted a prospect with this strategy once and he agreed that the money could be made available. He went on to tell me that his real reason for not going with the training was that he didn't want to admit to his boss that he lacked the foresight to budget for training and education. What began as a price objection resulted in a much different set of circumstances. I approached it from a different perspective. We scheduled our first training session for the next budget period. It was a timing and face-saving objection—not a price objection.

Future Order

If you find yourself in a situation where the real hesitation comes from lack of current budget, you may need to accept an order for the future. Some commitment at this point is better than no commitment at all. If you've exhausted all other possibilities, try this example:

> Mr. Buyer, even though you're unable to move on this idea during the current budget period, we can still get the wheels moving for the next one. If you give me your commitment, we can reserve the material for you. We won't ship or invoice you until your release date, but this at least gives us an opportunity to forecast production to meet your needs!

Many suppliers at this point have a contract to sign, require a purchase order, or want a deposit. It secures the order while ensuring the sincerity of the buyer. If the buyer is unwilling to commit at this point, there's a great likelihood he's not going to commit when the budget rolls around either. Probe deeper to determine the real objection.

Bottom-Line Response

Customers often assume that a savings in acquisition cost

means bottom-line savings. Sometimes this is true, but in most cases it's not. In many cases, the customer may save money in purchasing but has to make up for it in some other way. One customer saves freight charges by picking up an order. Another saves by purchasing bulk packages and subdividing internally. Another buys the product but does the assembling himself. In some cases a real savings is realized. In others, the savings is absorbed at least once and maybe twice by overhead. Here's a way to use this concept.

> Ms. Prospect, is the savings you're proposing going directly to your bottom line, or will it be absorbed once or maybe twice by overhead within your organization?

Your purpose is to cause the buyer to think. You want her to make a good business decision. In this case, paying a little more on the front end could be a great strategy.

In this section, you learned seventeen different strategies for dealing with price objections. Look beyond the wording of each of the examples. If these words aren't your words, change them but use the concept behind them. In most cases, it's nothing more than your asserting your quality, service, and support for the customer. If the buyer overlooks the quality, reinforce it. If he's forgotten how well you've treated him in the past, remind him. If he's disparaged the importance of service, illustrate how important it is. Sell the value you have at your disposal.

THREE COMMON PRICE OBJECTIONS

In this section, we'll examine the three most common price objections and suggest some ways to respond to these. Most of these concepts are explained fully in the previous section.

"I Don't Have the Money (Budget)!"

- Probe for discretionary money in other areas.
- Determine when the next budget period begins, and try for a future order.

- Use terms creatively. If your company has some lee-way here, you may be able to work out a payment schedule that is agreeable for everyone.
- Use the subtraction method and try to reduce the quality or service that you offer to meet the financial constraints imposed by the buyer.
- Shift the buyer's perspective from what the product will cost to what the product can earn for the buyer.
- Trial close. Find out whether or not the buyer would purchase if he had the funds available. If he wouldn't, dig a little deeper.
- Reverse the objection and demonstrate how going ahead with the decision makes sense.

"I Can Buy It Cheaper Somewhere Else!"

- Immediately without hesitation compare yourself with some other company that is more expensive. Your strategy is to position yourself in the middle— more buying decisions are made there. You might say this to the buyer: "Mr. Buyer, you can get it cheaper someplace else, and I also know of another company that charges more than we do."
- Cast doubt on what he's missing by not going with you. For example: "Mr. Buyer, no one is really in a better position than the competition to comment on the value of what they sell. If they're promoting a cheaper quality, I guess we must go along with their value assessment."
- Suggest that the competition meet your quality and service standards instead of your meeting their price.
- Weigh product differences against price differences. If your product is only 10 percent higher than the competition, discuss how many features and benefits the customer actually receives for 10 percent. Gener-ally, it's a wonderful deal for the customer and a prudent business decision.
- Reinforce uniqueness. Reiterate the unique strengths that your company offers.

- Trial close to determine who the buyer would go with if the prices were equal, and why.
- Sell loyalty. Elaborate on your past accomplishments. Remind the buyer how you've helped him in the past.
- Create a vital issues list. This is a list of questions you would like the buyer to consider before making a final decision to purchase from your competition. Naturally, these questions would highlight the weaknesses of the competition while drawing attention to your company's strengths. Make this list appear generic so the buyer doesn't perceive any negative selling against the competition. In presenting this to the buyer, explain that this is a shopper's guide you provide to all of your customers to ensure that you're meeting their needs.
- "If it's that good!" If the deal that the buyer has secured somewhere else is just that good, you may have to let him go. Simultaneously, tell the buyer that if for some reason the deal doesn't go the way he anticipates, you'd love to have an opportunity to service his needs.

"I Don't See Your Value!"

- Use analogies. Point out analogous purchases that enhance the buyer's bottom line through increased sales or reduced costs.
- Use success stories. Tell the buyer about other people who initially felt the same way but changed their minds after buying your product.
- Remind the buyer of the risk of cheapness.
- Point out the danger of buying dissonance.
- Alternate-advantage overload.

CHAPTER SUMMARY

In dealing with customer objections, you must be persistent. Persistence pays. Preparation also plays a major role in your success in dealing with objections. When you're prepared, you feel more confident being persistent and come across as more professional and convincing.

The three-step communications model you learned can be applied to all selling situations, but our emphasis was on dealing with price. In your response strategy, always focus on the value you bring to the buyer. You'll either make more money for him or save him money. Focus on the long-haul benefits of owning your product. With all of the prepared responses you're really saying, "Ms. Prospect, I understand that if I charge you too much, it will come back to haunt me. But I also understand that if I charge you too little, it will come back to haunt you!"

Mostly, be realistic. You'll lose some business because of price. There are shoppers out there whose only priority is getting a better price. They're compulsive bargain hunters, and unless you want to establish a flea-market reputation, avoid succumbing to the pressures. You don't want every order. You want every opportunity.

10
Lagniappe

W hen I lived in New Orleans, our newspaper had a special magazine supplement entitled "Lagniappe." It contained general interest features for the entire readership. *Lagniappe* is a word that means "something extra" or "more than you bargained for." That's what this chapter is all about. You're getting more than you bargained for! Because this is a general sales book, I wanted to include something for everyone. The topics in this chapter could each form an entire chapter by themselves. My objective in abbreviating these important areas is to highlight the key points that will enhance your sales presentation.

Specifically, I'll present some ideas on how you can become a more effective sales negotiator. We'll also examine how to discount creatively, raise your prices, and win competitive bids. We'll conclude the chapter with a few words of caution on the legal aspects of price.

NEGOTIATING IN SALES

Negotiating is the exchange of needs, wants, and desires by

two or more parties for the purpose of a win-win settlement. The reason people negotiate is so everyone feels he's gotten the best deal possible. Negotiating happens every day in almost every conceivable situation. When children ask to stay up later for a special TV show, they may offer to do extra chores around the house—they're negotiating. When my daughter offers my son a piece of her candy bar for a piece of his candy, she's negotiating. When you ask your boss for a raise, generally you're negotiating. When the customer asks for better prices, delivery, or terms, he's negotiating.

As you can see, negotiating isn't reserved for heads of state, labor representatives, or sports figures. We all negotiate. Our focus in this section is negotiation in sales. Specifically, we'll examine the role it plays regarding price.

Negotiating Tips

When negotiating with your buyer, remember these simple ideas.

- *Have a list of demands in advance.* Before you go into any negotiating session, know what things you must have and the things you're willing to trade off. Have two lists: "must haves" and "like to haves." The latter of the two is what you will most readily part with.
- *Knowledge equals power.* The more you know going into the session, the more powerful your position. Preparation directly affects the outcome of the negotiation. If you know more about your customer than he knows about you, you're in control. The opposite is also true. If he knows more about you than you know about him, he's in control. Take time to consider the impact of his paying less and receiving less. What will this do to his business? How will it influence his market position? Study the buyer's position and operate from a strategic vantage point. The more you know, the more profitably you sell.

- *Price is one criterion.* I've said this before. Discuss price as only one of several buying criteria. Generally, the buyer raises it as the only thing he wants. It's presented as the whole iceberg when in reality, it's just the tip. Flip the iceberg and uncover all of those driving forces that create the illusion that price is the most important variable.
- *Aim higher.* If conceding on price appears imminent, begin with a higher price and negotiate from there. This is not permission to gouge or deceive. Nature's law of gravity applies here. It's easier to negotiate a price downward than upward.
- *Use time patiently.* Most salespeople lose in negotiation because they violate this simple rule. Use time to your advantage. Selective foot-dragging can have a positive effect on the negotiation. The buyer is under the same, if not more critical, time demands as the salesperson. He must make a buying decision. When the salesperson prudently stalls, it increases buyer desire and the likelihood of securing a better price. When the buyer perceives your sense of urgency, he concludes that you're under the gun. Follow up with the buyer, but avoid appearing too anxious. Use as much time as the situation allows.
- *Invoke legitimacy.* A printed price list, a catalog, or a brochure with prices in it adds credibility to your presentation. When the buyer sees your information with a price printed on it, he's more willing to accept it. If your delivery and terms policies are included in a price list, refer to them also. The printed word is generally received as authoritative.
- *Use funny money.* Funny money is sometimes referred to as soft dollars. It represents an indirect cost to the bottom line and is often difficult to make tangible. Funny money could be your time, free training for the buyer's employees when they purchase equipment, or free maintenance for a specified period of time. Rather than conceding on a better

price, look for ways to handle the price issue with funny money. Offer installation assistance at no charge. Offer the services of your research and development department to help solve a pressing quality problem the buyer is experiencing with the product. Give a distributor additional literature that has been customized.

Some manufacturing companies will offer their distributors free goods instead of a cash rebate. This is funny money. It makes sense to use this approach for two reasons. First, your cost of goods is cheaper than your cost of money. One thousand dollars' worth of inventory may cost you only five hundred dollars, but you're still getting one thousand dollars' worth of good will. Second, the distributor must sell the goods, which means he's out promoting you in the market. Funny money gives the customer the extras he wants and allows you to maintain profitability and pricing integrity.

- *Negotiate the unnegotiable.* Many times buyers tell us that since the budget has been established it is no longer negotiable. That just isn't true. Have you ever heard someone say, "This is my final offer," and then they accept something less? A good rule of thumb to use is that anything that's been negotiated once can be renegotiated again and again. Budgets are the result of an internally negotiated settlement. They can be renegotiated. Don't be fooled by the apparent finality of this tactic.
- *Use your ears.* The negotiator who listens more than he talks wins more positions. In an effort to sell your position, you may volunteer too much information. Your goal in negotiating is to tell the other person only enough to make your point. Let the other negotiator have the talking initiative. Remember the World War II admonishment, "Loose lips sink ships!"
- *Determine the buyer's position early.* In the needs-

analysis phase of the sale, determine the three most important buying criteria. Try to understand the buyer's needs in terms of absolutes and areas of flexibility. Mentally weigh the buyer's list of needs and demands against your own list of demands. Target early agreement on his major points so that the buying decision is nothing more than working out minor details.

- *Flip the iceberg.* In the negotiation process, price generally becomes the focal point. However, in most cases it's just the tip of the iceberg. Our task in the negotiating process is to uncover all of those driving forces beneath the surface to understand why price is so important. A failure to uncover these needs diminishes the likelihood of selling more profitably. Earlier I said that knowledge is power. If the buyer knows more than you about what is below the surface, he's in control. If you know as much as he does, you're on equal footing.

- *Lagniappe.* When the negotiation process is complete, throw in a little something extra for the buyer. You want him to feel he received extra value. It doesn't need to be anything major—just a little freebie to show you care. My wife and I stopped at a specialty candy shop in St. Louis. My wife purchased a bag of assorted hard candies for the children, and after the clerk weighed the bag and charged us, he threw in a handful of candy as lagniappe. It was unprompted and unexpected. I'm sure that the price of that freebie is included in the regular price of the candy. But it sure felt great to get more than we expected!

Negotiating Areas

In negotiations with your buyer, there are several options available other than price. Many times, the buyer relents on price for some other concession. Other times, giving a slightly better price to the buyer makes sense for a different commitment on his part. What are these negotiating options?

- *Specifications change.* One option is the specifications of your product or the buyer's needs. Can your buyer accept less quality, service, or delivery to achieve his buying goal? Can you change your specs to meet the buyer's needs for quality and price? If he wants less, how can you give it to him? If your product is overengineered to meet the customer's needs, you may need to create the perception of less value with a less expensive alternative. Private label and generic label products often accomplish this even though the quality is the same as a brand name item. Look for ways to offer a streamlined alternative without the frills, or look for ways to get the buyer to change his specs.
- *Drop shipment.* Some companies ship directly from the manufacturer to the buyer to avoid extra handling. The packaging may not be ideal and delivery time somewhat protracted, but it generally involves a savings to the supplier that can be passed along. The real value of a drop shipment is that it doesn't tarnish the image of the product. You're not setting a precedent for less-expensive goods. Rather, you're establishing a precedent for delivery charges. A spin-off benefit of drop shipment is that the normal delays in transit highlight the value of your normal stocking and delivery. The buyer experiences a loss of the good service that he's accustomed to.
- *Terms.* When interest rates fluctuate, terms become more or less desirable. A general rule of thumb for most companies is to take the discount and pay early. Normal terms are 2 percent for ten days—net 30 percent. This means you receive a 2 percent discount if you pay the invoice within ten days. I've heard all types of creative ideas for discounting with terms: 5

percent to prepay your order, 3 percent COD, ninety days is the same as cash. Perhaps the most startling I've heard is 3 percent for forty-five days. This is in an industry where the suppliers sell to small companies. Small companies generally have cash flow problems which result in their not paying on time. Suppliers have resorted to offering an additional discount to receive their payment within six weeks!

- *Increased volume.* When the buyer asks for a better price, increasing the size of the order may be prudent strategy. I say *may* because you must consider the impact of the discount. Ask yourself some questions about the larger volume: "Can we handle the additional low-profit volume without adversely affecting the service to our other customers?" Maybe your company cannot handle the increased capacity. Ask, "Do we really want to 'give away' a larger quantity of our goods at lower margins?" Another question to ask is "Does this volume discount encourage the buyer to think in these terms all the time?" Maybe he'll form a buying consortium with the other more profitable customers to take advantage of this volume all the time. The principle of "making it up in volume" that you learned in Economics 101 failed to raise these questions. There's one thing worse than selling a product at a discount—selling a lot of that product at a discount.

- *Longer commitment.* Another option when negotiating is to seek a longer commitment period for a contract. You may be unable to lower your current prices, but it's possible for you to hold them at the current level for an extended period. Another possibility is to offer a smaller discount than the buyer originally wanted, but for a longer period.

- *Additional items.* If you find yourself in a position where a discount is inevitable, add more items to the contract. The items you add are naturally the more profitable ones you sell. Another option is to extend a

smaller discount to a broader range of products.
Evaluate the buyer's purchasing habits before tender-
ing your offer. The ideal solution is the one that
enables you to maximize across-the-board margins
while simultaneously giving the buyer a fair price.

- *Freight.* Companies have used freight as a negotiating point for years. Either the supplier pays freight or
  the buyer pays the freight. The supplier might pay
  the freight and invoice the buyer with extended
  terms. Another possibility is to arrange for the buyer
  to pick up the inventory himself. You could also have
  a tiered freight-and-delivery charge for "extra-quick"
  or "hotshot" deliveries and a different charge for
  routine deliveries.

- *Referrals.* You may negotiate a bird-dog credit program as part of your contract. When the buyer refers
  other people (within his company or outside of it),
  you offer him a credit for free goods. Another way to
  tie referrals to a contract is to tell the buyer his
  discount is tied to giving you referrals to other locations. If you must relent on price, at least get some
  names of some prospects for your goods. Getting
  referrals and getting discounts are unrelated concepts, but the idea is to get something back for the
  discount you've offered.

- *Packaging change.* If the buyer wants a better price,
  perhaps you can offer to make a change in the way
  your product is packaged. A more convenient packaging size might induce the buyer to spend a little
  more for your product. If you currently subdivide
  your products into smaller units, offer a bulk package. If you're reducing the number of steps it takes to
  sell your goods, you can pass that savings on to the
  buyer and still maintain your profitability on the
  sale.

Your goal in negotiation is to maximize your position
while giving the buyer the fairest deal possible. When both

parties feel they have struck a fair deal, it's a win-win settlement. When one of the parties feels he's given up too much, it's a win-lose or lose-win settlement. Since you're negotiating a relationship with your potential customer, your goal is to ensure that the buyer walks away from the table satisfied that he got the best deal possible. This doesn't imply the cheapest price. It means the best overall value for his money: service, delivery, quality, and so on.

DISCOUNTING

Discounting is an inevitable part of selling. If you're in sales long enough, sooner or later it's going to happen. Your objective in discounting is to cut your prices without cutting your throat. Develop a strategy for your discounts. Here are a few simple tips to remember when discounting.

- *Time limit.* Whenever you offer special pricing, create a sense of urgency and finality. The buyer must understand that your discount is good only for a specified period of time. Your deadline creates a greater sense of buyer desire via urgency. Because the buyer sees the imminent demise of his discounted price, he understands that discounting is not your usual way of doing business.
- *Negotiate individually.* Within the guidelines of the law, negotiate each discount separately. Don't offer the same discount across the board unless the buying habits are exactly the same. If you're selling through wholesalers, dealers, or distributors, it's a different story because they require a standard discount. Negotiate individually when you're dealing with the end-user.
- *Don't set precedents.* I don't know very many people who would pay sticker price for a new car. I also know very few people who would pay the asking price for a home. The reason is the precedent has been set. Most people know that you don't need to

pay full price, and once the precedent has been set, it's tough to change a buyer's behavior. Remember this when you sell your goods. Rather than set a dangerous precedent by discounting, you're better off losing one order than destroying the profit potential on all future orders.

- *Get more down the street.* If you can sell your goods somewhere else for a higher price, why sell them cheaper to this buyer? There would need to be some unusual and extenuating circumstances to make such a discount a prudent business decision. A simple rule of thumb to follow is: why give it away when someone else is willing to pay?

- *Watch your image.* Cutting your price doesn't appear to be a good business strategy if it damages your image. If your organization has invested substantial resources in positioning your product and company, discounting or cutting your prices can tarnish this image. Consider the impact of heavy discounting on your existing customers. If you've charged more all along and then begin discounting, it sends a negative message. You're saying that you've been gouging the customers in the past. In many cases, it's much better to lose a sale than lose your credibility as a supplier and market leader.

- *Don't compound bad decisions.* Don't let an unscrupulous competitor lure you into a price battle. Worse than that, don't let a bad business decision by a competitor draw you into a battle over price. If your competition is making bad business decisions, let them. It's not your place to match their ignorance tit for tat. Unless you want to go down the tubes with them, keep your margins high. You may lose an occasional order, but you'll win in the end. Think long-term and make your decisions for the long haul.

- *Consider the increase in sales.* In the first chapter, I demonstrated the tremendous increase in sales you need to compensate for a 15 percent discount to your customer. You need a 43 percent increase in sales to sustain the profit contribution to the bottom line. If you cut your prices 15 percent, are you prepared to increase your sales volume by that much? It seems like a lot of work to just stay at your current level.

- *Know when to discount.* There are times when it makes sense to discount. Scrutinize the situation by using the above suggestions, and then make your decision. Here are some additional thoughts on discounting. It might make sense to discount when . . .
    1. You're in a mature market and very few product changes are happening.
    2. You're controlling the market and you want to keep the competition out. It becomes a proactive strategy: "Head 'em off at the pass!"
    3. You have very little need to promote or advertise. Some of these savings can be passed along to the end-user to thwart competitive moves into your market.
    4. You're attempting to draw buyers into your domain. A loss leader makes sense when the buyer purchases additional items from you that more than compensate for what you've lost. Retailers do this more often than commercial sellers do.
    5. You're able to turn your inventory quickly or you're overstocked and need to move some to make room for additional products.

WHAT PRICE TO CHARGE?

There are ways to determine if you're charging too much or too little. Here are some ideas you can use for guidelines.

You're Not Charging Enough When . . .

- Sales remain constant or grow when your gross profit is slipping.

- Buyers don't complain about your price. Use the 20 percent rule. If one-fifth of your buyers don't complain, you're probably underpriced.
- Buyers have quit asking your prices before they purchase.
- Price shoppers in your industry begin flocking to your door for no apparent reason.
- Current customers begin talking about how smart your management is to be able to operate a company so efficiently.
- You haven't raised prices during an inflationary period.
- You experience an influx of new business that is inexplicable according to the normal rules of supply and demand.
- Buyers begin hoarding and buying as much as they can from you.

You're Charging Too Much When . . .

- You receive more price complaints than in the past— more than 20 percent of your customers complain.
- Profitability increases but sales are dropping or remaining flat.
- Customers begin to scrutinize your price to determine what goes into it and what you're missing.
- Your competitors' business is growing without much effort on their part.
- Your sales cycle increases. It takes longer to sell your product.
- The buyer asks for competitive bids.
- Known quality shoppers begin asking you to justify your prices.

Adjusting your prices up or down requires something more than a judgment call or intuition on your part. Before you offer special pricing, make sure that it fits into your whole business strategy.

COMPETITIVE BIDDING

This is one of the most perplexing and intimidating aspects of sales for most people. Buyers offer hopes for substantial contracts and then choose items from various quotes, leaving questionable margins for suppliers. A buyer once told a group of salespeople in a training session that "the easiest way to get rid of a salesperson is to ask him to give me a quote on something! He generally leaves feeling optimistic, when in fact I've just stalled him!" Even though this has probably happened to each of us, there are legitimate requests for quotations.

It has been my experience with salespeople that most of them get pretty intimidated by the buyer when it's time to quote something. Part of the reason is that you, the salesperson, don't fully understand your rights in that situation. This is what I call the "Bill of Rights for Salespeople" during quotations and proposals.

Right #1: Before making the quote, you're entitled to talk with relevant parties (end-users, decision makers, etc.) who will be involved in the selection process. Otherwise, it's a shot in the dark. If you were a doctor, would you prescribe without seeing the patient? Probably you wouldn't. If the buyer gives you any problems, use this analogy. Common sense is on your side. If the buyer is that uncooperative before the sale, can you imagine how uncooperative he'll be after the sale? No price is good enough! No delivery soon enough! No service good enough! Do you want every order opportunity?

Right #2: You have a right to know all of the selection criteria that will be used in making the final decision. Would you ever gamble away your money in a Las Vegas card game and not know all the rules? Of course you wouldn't.

However, in sales when you don't fully know the rules before you quote, you're gambling with your time and margins. Find out in advance the relative importance of price, delivery, responsiveness, and technical support.

Right #3: You have a right to know with whom you're competing. Explain to the buyer that you expect nothing more than the same courtesy he would expect from his customers. Explain that you're interested in maintaining your margins while offering a fair deal and that you need some competitive information in order to do that. Once you discover who your competition is, you may decide to bid extremely high just to send a strong message to the price-oriented supplier.

Right #4: You have a right for a bid recap after the contract has been awarded. Explain to the buyer up front that one of your conditions is that you receive at least an oral summary of how you compared with other bidders. You may not be able to get specific numbers, but you may be able to get a ballpark percentage.

If any of these personal rights seem extreme or aggressive to you, consider the options. You're called into a buyer's office because he wants you to quote a price on something. Since you haven't called here much in the past, you're unsure of what they do. You ask permission to speak to some of the end-users but are declined permission. The buyer tells you that everything is handled through him. He gives you scanty information about their needs but can't answer any of the technical questions that might give you a strategic advantage in bidding. When you ask what selection criteria are used for buying decisions, he says, "The usual: price, quality, and delivery!" The buyer then informs you that there are three other vendors competing with you but he fails to tell you who they are. In his words, "Our policy is not to tell you who you're competing with. Just give us your best price and we'll let you know if you win!" When you ask about the bid recap the buyer says that all you'll know is who won and nothing more.

If the buyer treats you this way going into a quote, how do you think he'll treat you after you get the business? Are you sure you want to do business with him? Is the aggravation factor worth the profit? You have rights as a salesperson. When you don't respect yourself, buyers won't respect you. If you believe in your rights and assert them, your buyers will respect you as a businessperson and as a fellow human being.

When you receive a request for quotation, you need to have a strategy. It makes sense to subdivide your strategy into three parts: before the quote, submission, and recap activities.

Before the Quote

- Determine the actual buying authority before you submit your quote. Find out who will have some impact on the buying decision and try to visit with as many people as possible before the contract is awarded.
- If board approval is part of the procedure, try to meet with individual board members. Develop some loyalties. Try to establish at least one strong ally on the board who will speak candidly in your defense. This person can also be your sounding board for you to gain substantial feedback.
- Get the buyer to write the quote according to your specifications. This works especially well when your product has several unique features and benefits that the competition's doesn't have. Generally, you can accomplish this when you have gained thorough account penetration with the end-users.
- Gather enough relevant information. You may want

to standardize this by developing a quote fact sheet containing the following information:

1. Selection criteria for products and vendors.
2. Timetable for decision making and the delivery of products and services.
3. Information regarding your competition for this piece of business.
4. Bidding history of this account. For example, who got this business in the past, and at what level? Did the buyer order as much as he originally stated in the quote? How satisfied is the buyer with previous suppliers?
5. How do terms affect the buying decision?
6. Does the supplier's location make a difference to the buyer?

- Ask if you can get the business even if you're not the least expensive.
- Ask what it would take for the buyer not to go out for a competitive quote.
- When designing your proposal, try to make it as unique as possible. Use a quality binder. Begin with a summary sheet of the buyer's needs. Include several no-charge items such as free training, service, and follow-up. Embellish this section of no-charge items: it creates a greater perception of value. Include guarantees and testimonials. Be sure to demonstrate in the proposal how your product specifically addresses the buyer's needs. Also, put a time limit on the quote to avoid delays on the other end.

Submitting the Quote

- Demonstrate how you arrived at your price. Use the review-needs/project-ownership technique that appears in the chapter on the presentation stage.
- Deliver the proposal personally so that you can answer any questions that may surface.
- Elaborate on the no-charge items and stress the guarantees you offer.

- Ask subtle questions that bring immediate feedback on how you compare with the competition.
- Seek active buyer involvement to draw out any concerns or doubts he has.

Recapping Your Bid

- Get feedback immediately following the bid opening.
- Talk to as many people as possible. Sometimes an end-user paints a much different picture from the one buyers do.
- Pinpoint the actual selection criteria that was used to make the decision.
- Discover who got the bid and at what price level.
- Ask the buyer, "What could we have done differently with our quote to receive your business?"
- Send a recap letter to the buyer thanking him for an opportunity to quote. Reaffirm your interest in his business and tell him that you'll continue to honor your terms on the proposal until the "honeymoon period" with the new supplier is over. Give it about ninety days.
- Schedule regular follow-up calls to determine his satisfaction level with his current vendor. Determine the competition's ability to meet the buyer's needs and check to see how the buyer is preparing to meet his future needs.

Quoting doesn't need to be a painful or intimidating situation. Have a strategy for your proposals and go the extra step to make yours appear unique. If you don't get the business, maintain periodic contact because you might be able to get some peripheral business at higher profitability than your original quote reflected.

RAISING PRICES

Your heart is racing, you feel an emptiness in your stomach, your palms are sweaty, and when you speak there's a tremor in your voice. My guess is that you're sitting across the desk from a current customer justifying a price increase. It's unrealistic to expect the customer to be thrilled at a price increase. Your best strategy is to be prepared to use all of the tools available to you. For your organization to survive, it must raise its prices periodically.

When to Raise Prices

- Use the bandwagon approach. If your competitors raise their prices on January 1, it makes sense for you to do so at that same time. The buyers can then spread their misery over several vendors.
- Quarterly increases are about as often as you want to raise your prices unless you're in an industry where prices change daily. For example, the stock market and commodities-related businesses fluctuate almost hourly. Unless you're in that type of situation you're better off to raise your prices less frequently.
- Raise your prices when your customer's business is doing well. It's more difficult for the customer to complain of eroding profit margins when his have increased. The best place to determine this is to watch the Dun and Bradstreet reports on your customers. When your customers' profits go up, raise your prices.
- Tie your price increases to government reports of inflation. When the inflation index demonstrates that the cost of living has increased, it's difficult to argue with a vendor that he shouldn't raise prices to cover his costs. Good businesspeople recognize this fact.
- Raise your prices when your customers stop complaining about or questioning your price.
- When the supply-and-demand relationship is in your favor, raise your prices. If there's a scarcity of your products, don't give them away. If someone will pay

more for your products, don't sell them to a price shopper. Raise the prices and court the buyer who recognizes your value.

How to Raise Prices

- Don't raise your price too much at any given time. Customers are sensitive to gouging. If you're under-priced to begin with, you need to get your prices into the competitive ballpark. Raise them gradually and more often. Think about parity with your competition over the long haul. Don't try to make it up in one movement.
- When raising prices in one area, lower something else at the same time. Naturally, the prices you want to lower are those slow-moving items that will probably be deleted shortly anyhow. Be selective in the prices you lower; make it a sound business decision.
- Give your key accounts plenty of advance notice. On certain items you may even want a grandfather clause that enables them to purchase for ninety days at the old pricing. Protect your good customers and help them adjust by allowing them to anticipate these trends. Give them enough notice that they're able to pass along the increase in some fashion.
- Justify the increase with tangible reasons. Demonstrate how your cost of doing business has increased over the time period you're discussing. It's a good opportunity for you to discuss all of the special things you've done for the customer that were above and beyond the call of duty. Cite how specific instances actually cost your organization something.
- You may even want to throw in something extra to sweeten the deal for the customer: extra terms for the first three months of the increase, free delivery on the next order, price protection on selected items, or a change in returned goods policy.

Creative Profit-Building Ideas

You can raise your prices surreptitiously and increase profitability if you use creative strategies. Here are some ideas to get you started.

- Increase your minimum order size. This reduces your administrative costs while increasing the total profit dollars contributed to the bottom line.
- Start charging for delivery, service calls, training, repairs, samples, etc.
- Charge for installation or delivery consultation.
- If the job requires overtime at your plant, pass these extra costs along to the customer.
- Produce, inventory, and sell fewer of the low-margin items. Create less demand for them in the marketplace.
- Build escalation clauses into your contracts. If your costs increase, your selling price does also.
- Actively look for ways to cut costs internally without sacrificing the quality of the product or the service level you've achieved.

LEGAL CONSIDERATIONS

As a caveat to you, please be aware of the legal ramifications of pricing. The laws governing fair play and equitable pricing are straightforward. If there's any doubt about the legality of the prices you charge or the discount schedules you offer, get legal counsel before submitting the prices to your buyer. Be cautious so you don't collude with other vendors. Price fixing brings stiff penalties under the law.

These laws are designed to protect everyone, you as well as the buyer. They protect you from less scrupulous vendors and protect the buyer from being gouged. Consult an attorney specifically on these laws: the Sherman Antitrust Act and the Clayton Act (Robinson-Patman Amendment).

This book is not intended to offer you legal advice on price setting. Rather, its purpose is to provide you with some creative ideas and concepts to boost your profitability.

CHAPTER SUMMARY

Salespeople need to become better negotiators. Because they don't fully realize how powerful they are, salespeople generally negotiate from a position of weakness. You're stronger than you know. You're more powerful than you know. Organizing yourself before going into the negotiation will build your self-confidence. Have a list of those things you must have and those things you'd like to have. Know your demands in advance.

Discounting is sometimes a prudent business strategy. And that's the key: it is a strategy. If offering the buyer a discount is not part of your overall business strategy, then question the effectiveness of using it. Cutting your prices should be part of your overall plan—not instant gratification of a buyer's request.

Competitive bidding and submitting proposals can be intimidating if you're unaccustomed to asserting your rights. You have rights as a professional and owe it to yourself to assert them. When quoting, remember that you need extensive up-front information regarding buying habits or selection criteria. Be sure to submit the proposal personally and present it in its best light. Recap as soon as possible after the quote. Use this information to build your own competitive intelligence file and feed it back to your marketing department so that everyone can benefit from it.

Raising prices requires a unique blend of tact, diplomacy, and foresight. You must raise them at the right moment using a spoonful of sugar to make the increase go down more easily.

Everyone needs to be cognizant of the legal ramifications of pricing. You can find yourself and your company in more trouble than you ever anticipated if you're unaware of the legal issues. When in doubt, check it out.

11
Have You Hugged Your Customers Lately?

Have you hugged your customer lately?
Have you told 'em that you care?
Have you reached out boldly . . .
And said, "We know you're there"?

What have you said?
What have you done?
How have you hugged 'em
And said, "You're number one"?

In a crazy, mixed-up, me-first world
Where greed is the game to play,
Have you hugged your customer lately
And said, "In our book you're OK"?

When the well is dry,
And your hopes are low,
And your business has gone to pot . . .
You don't have to look far
Just beyond your nose
'Cause you've hugged your customer not.

Have you taken 'em for granted,
Expecting to rule the roost?
Or have you hugged 'em fondly
And given your sales a boost?

I'm a hugger, a plugger, and a big-league slugger
Because I follow this simple rule.
If I want to succeed and make my mark
I just live like a huggin' fool.

Tom Reilly, 1985

S ome time ago a salesperson gave me a bumper sticker that said, "Have you hugged your salesperson lately?" This was a clever take-off on a popular theme. I hung the bumper sticker in my training center and received numerous positive comments from the salespeople who attended my seminars. Their comments and the constant reminder hanging in my office awakened my interest in "hugging."

I began looking around and saw a variety of these stickers on cars: "Have you hugged your lawyer, doctor, accountant, secretary, electrician, etc., today?" Everyone wants to be hugged! It occurred to me that we've become a fairly egocentric society, more concerned with receiving hugs than giving them. I speculated how that might influence the business community. Then it dawned on me. Maybe we should launch a hugging campaign for our customers.

I coupled this newly discovered insight with something I'd observed for some time. Most companies spend more money pursuing new business than they do keeping existing customers satisfied. In fact, one study claims that it costs companies six times as much to secure a new customer than it does to keep one satisfied. It occurred to me that the quickest way to positively influence your bottom line is to keep customers happy.

The logic also follows that happy customers are willing to pay a little more for goods and services than unhappy customers are. This fits well within the value-oriented sales philosophy. One way to keep your customer happy and satisfied is to actively seek ways to add value to what you sell. Create opportunities to hug your customer.

I define hugging as the amount of consistent, quality attention you give your customers. It is both a quantitive and a qualitive concept. Delivering consistent attention is a quantitive measurement indicative of how often you do it. Your thoroughness, level of coverage, depth of concern, genuine appreciation, and so on are qualitive measurements of hugging.

Hugging should occur at all levels in an organization. Does your security guard greet people as they enter your location, or is he guarding? Does your switchboard operator sound like she had a bad night, or does she welcome customers' inquiries? How do your customer-service people work with customers? Does the customer feel more frustrated or satisfied after dealing with them? How do your management personnel hug your customers? Are they sincere, or do they just pay lip service to a hugging philosophy? The impact is simple. If you don't hug your customer at every point of contact, you don't embrace a value-oriented sales philosophy.

This chapter is about the danger signals that indicate when your customer is ready to leave you for someone else. You'll relive some of the excuses you've heard around your office for not hugging. And not to leave you hanging there, I'll offer a bonanza of hugging ideas to get you started.

WHY SHOULD I HUG THE CUSTOMER?

Hugging your customer makes you the recipient of a host of benefits. Look at a few:

- Hugging encourages trust because the customer perceives more genuine concern on your part for his welfare. He knows you're interested in more than just his money.
- Because you're delivering consistent attention, the

customer feels obliged to continue to award you the business you've earned.

- Hugging means you're knowledgeable about what's going on with the customer. You stay abreast of vital information that could signal a sales opportunity.
- Huggers experience greater account control because of their knowledge and influence. They also have a lower attrition rate among their customers. Satisfied customers rarely switch vendors.
- Hugging generally results in a feeling of satisfaction that you've done your best and gone the extra step. You're living a sense of commitment that few people experience.

The impact of not hugging is obvious. When you don't hug your customer, you open the door for someone else to do it. You miss valuable feedback: information on how your product works, sales leads, or new opportunities for your company. Not hugging means you fail to nip problems in the bud because your contact level is shallow. The most potentially dangerous consequence of not hugging is the image you project in the marketplace. You tell customers that you don't care enough to show your appreciation. Can you afford that type of reputation?

DANGER SIGNALS

Many employees and managers think they're hugging when they're not. Here's a checklist of the signals customers send your way to indicate waning interest in your company.

Corporate Headache

"I'm sorry honey, I've got a headache—not tonight!" Some people hear this at home as a signal that things aren't as peachy as they could be. The same thing could be said for business. You call for an appointment, make a lunch or dinner engagement, or in some other way attempt to meet with your customer, and you hear a series of excuses why the customer is unable to meet: "I'm so sorry! You see, we're swamped, and I just can't shake loose!" "Could you call me back in a few weeks (or months)?" "I'd love to go to lunch but I have a root canal scheduled!" In each case, the customer has the "corporate headache." He doesn't want to meet with you so he creates excuses. If you hear these excuses every time you call, check your hugging strategy.

Unrequited Love

How sad we are when our affections for another person are not returned! Who can forget the first unrequited crush in grammar or high school? It was the end of the world. Unfortunately, we experience this in business also. The customer fails to return your phone calls, letters are unanswered, and special favors for the customer go unacknowledged. You have become the victim of your own hugging deficit. Chances are the customer has found someone else who's more responsive to his needs. Your actions are perceived as "too little, too late"!

Freudian Slip

Imagine the relationships that have been destroyed by the utterance of the wrong name at the wrong time. A slip of the "business tongue" could signal the demise of your sales. Your customer may slip and use a competitor's name when talking to you. He offers you a cup of coffee—in your competitor's mug! He uses the competitor's literature to explain what he wants in a product. Some of these actions might be inadvertent by the customer—others may be intentional.

Time Takes Its Toll

Time begins working against you. You're left on hold longer than usual, and then the customer's secretary tells you he'll call back later. You're left waiting in the lobby for what seems to be an eternity. Orders trickle in, accounts receivable slow down, and the customer complaints increase. The customer is using time to vent his frustration—a reflection of your hugging deficit.

Pain Versus Gain

Your number one danger signal is when you begin to perceive the customer as a pain rather than a gain. The phone rings and you see this as an interruption rather than an opportunity. A new prospect contacts you and you see this as one more bit of aggravation for you to handle. Your vision is muddled and your attitude sour. That mental set brings you more problems than you ever anticipated. Your attitude is a virus so wildly out of control that it will destroy everything in its path. Chances are you've let the altitude of your success affect your attitude of success. It's time for an attitude adjustment and a recommitment to a value-oriented philosophy.

If you've experienced any of these danger signals, it's time to check your hugging philosophy and action plan; maybe you're bugging instead of hugging your customer.

TWENTY-ONE WAYS TO GET DIVORCED FROM YOUR CUSTOMER

I've talked with hundreds of salespeople about their company's philosophy on hugging and accumulated a list of reasons why companies don't hug. In most cases, these reasons are excuses or rationalizations for the lack of a fully developed business plan. See if you recognize anything on this list that might describe your company.

- Not caring enough to hug.
- Assuming the customer doesn't want or need to be hugged.
- A personality conflict with the customer precludes hugging.

- A product-driven rather than customer-driven business philosophy.
- A philosophy that you can't please everyone all the time anyway, so why try?
- Fear of bad results: "We don't want to hear what the customer has to say."
- Fear of being seen as a pest.
- Fear of becoming too good of friends with the customer and giving too much service.
- Fear of having your intentions misread.
- Greener pastures await us!
- The customer is perceived as small potatoes.
- Company policy dictates that we pursue new business to the exclusion of servicing existing customers.
- Don't know how to hug.
- Don't have time to hug.
- It's too expensive to hug!
- Turnover is so high we lack the personnel to hug.
- Lack of confidence in our product, company, and selves.
- One-time sale mentality: "We sell fast and get out—there's nothing else we can do for them."
- There's no challenge in hugging: "We already have the business."
- It's-not-broke-so-don't-fix-it philosophy—leave well enough alone.
- The take-'em-for-granted philosophy, whereby the customer calls you if he has a problem.

Some of these may appear to be legitimate, but in most cases they're excuses. Even with limited resources, can you really afford not to hug your customer on a regular basis?

HOW TO HUG YOUR CUSTOMERS

To become a hugger, plugger, and big-league slugger, follow this game plan. Begin with the hugging attitude. Recognize the importance of giving consistent quality attention to your customer. Develop an attitude of gratitude for the business you've earned. Don't let the altitude of your success affect your attitude of success. Be grateful and count your blessings. Accept the reality that you're in business because of and for your customers. Their satisfaction level and your bottom line are directly related.

Plan your hugging awareness. Develop a strategic marketing plan that includes a consistent effort directed toward customer satisfaction. Schedule regular follow-up meetings with customers to assure their satisfaction with your products or services. Plan a campaign that includes all of your customers to avoid having someone feel slighted. You may not give all your customers the same amount of attention, but you can still service all of them.

Communicate with your customers regularly. Actions speak louder than words. Let them know through your actions that you mean business. Use your ears twice as much as your mouth. Listen to what your customers say and respond to it. Give them the opportunity to sing your praises as well as vent their spleen.

A BONANZA OF HUGGING IDEAS

This is a list of some creative things I've seen companies do to hug their customers. Its purpose is to stimulate your creative juices once you've seen what others have done.

- Send special cards for different occasions.
- Have a scheduled "Hugging Blitz"—e.g., one day per quarter when each salesperson gets on the phone and calls each existing customer to thank him for his business.
- Build hugging into your business plan: "Don't forget to till the soil for existing crops while planting new seeds."
- Visit the customer in person.
- Get to know him personally.
- Say thanks (notes/orally) or send gifts of appreciation.

- Offer expert help in another area of his business.
- Make the customer a hero 365 days per year.
- Call often.
- Hold cocktail parties and open houses for customers.
- Keep them abreast of changes in policies, and why, and give them plenty of advance notice.
- Conduct customer-satisfaction surveys.
- Use specialty advertising gifts.
- Offer free goods or samples that will help.
- Have a monthly dinner raffle: put the customer's name in a fishbowl.
- Compliment them.
- Hold monthly roundtable discussions.
- Do business with them; buy their products.
- Send business their way by referrals.
- Use entertainment wisely—lunches and dinners.
- Send congratulations for family and personal achievements.
- Return phone calls promptly or at least have an assistant call back and say when you'll return the call.
- Be easily accessible to the customer and maybe even have a direct-dial number that the customer can use—"Hot Line for Hot Customers."
- Give your home phone number for emergency situations.
- Recommend their product to others and then pass the lead along.
- Have customer councils give you scheduled feedback.
- Hold hands to assuage buyer remorse.
- Keep them informed of industry trends.
- Offer no-charge favors in service.
- Institute hugging awareness campaigns throughout your entire company.
- Ask this question: "What is the most I can do today for the customer?"
- Develop a newsletter for customers.
- Send them magazine articles of general interest.
- Ask how they want to be hugged.

- Ask what they expect of you.
- Set time aside each week to hug: make it a high priority and schedule other things around it.

CHAPTER SUMMARY

Hugging requires a consistent effort on your part. It's a philosophy that must be embraced at every level in your organization. A negligent attitude at the top doesn't trickle down—it's a downpour! Hugging offers you as many wonderful opportunities as not hugging offers potentially dangerous outcomes. Develop your hugging attitude, plan your strategy, and then communicate it to your customers.

12
Where Do I Go from Here?

From the moment you opened this book, you've taken a risk. You've risked being influenced by what you've read, and I appreciate that risk. Now there's a much greater risk ahead of you: the risk of implementing what you've learned.

It's been written that there is no heavier burden than a great opportunity. The task ahead of you represents either a burden or an opportunity depending upon your perspective. With this opportunity comes risk, and with risk comes fear: fear of the known; fear of the unknown; fear of what may happen; or worse yet, a fear of what may not happen.

As I write these final words, I'm asking that you accept the challenge ahead of you. I'm asking that you risk success as well as failure. I'm asking that you pursue your duty to yourself and to your company by becoming a value-added salesperson. Risk the value-added approach. Risk selling more profitably. Risk rising to the top of your profession. And mostly, risk reaching your full potential!

Robert Schuller has been quoted as saying, "I would rather attempt a great many things in this world and fail

than to attempt nothing and succeed!" Will you risk great-
ness in your life?

Good luck and God bless!

For more information from Tom Reilly on sales techniques
contact:

Sales Motivational Services
171 Chesterfield Industrial Boulevard
Chesterfield, MO 63005-1219
(314) 537-3360
(800) 727-0026